145955 Designed and Produced by Wakefield Council. Communications 11/15 ♻recycle

70   D0490054

MAIN LINE
STEAM
IN THE 1980s

ROGER SIVITER
ARPS

SUTTON PUBLISHING

First published in 2003 by
Sutton Publishing Limited · Phoenix Mill
Thrupp · Stroud · Gloucestershire · GL5 2BU

British Library Cataloguing in Publication Data
A catalogue record for this book is available from the British Library.

ISBN 0-7509-3391-7

Title page photograph: LMS 'Black Five' 4–6–0 No. 5407 climbs the steep gradient at Carnforth East
junction and heads for Hellifield with the bottom section of the northbound 'Cumbrian Mountain
Pullman' on 20 February 1982. At Hellifield, LMS Coronation Pacific No. 46229 *Duchess of Hamilton*
will replace No. 5407 for the 72-mile journey over the former Midland Railway Settle & Carlisle route
to Carlisle.

LNER A4 Pacific No. 4468 *Mallard* tops Ais Gill summit on the Settle & Carlisle line with a
southbound special on Saturday 27 August 1988.

Typeset in 10/12 pt Palatino.
Typesetting and origination by
Sutton Publishing Limited.
Printed and bound in England by
J.H. Haynes & Co. Ltd, Sparkford.

Contents

On 23 May 1987, Castle Class 4–6–0 No. 7029 *Clun Castle* passes a fine array of GWR semaphore signals as it approaches High Wycombe station with a 'Traintours Charter' return special from London Marylebone to Birmingham Tyseley, Tyseley shed/museum being the home of No. 7029.

Although *Clun Castle* is always regarded as a GWR locomotive (the Castle Class was first introduced on the GWR in 1923 to a design by C.B. Collett), No. 7029 was built at Swindon in BR days, and was completed in May 1950.

Arguably the most famous locomotive in the world, LNER Class A3 Pacific No. 4472 *Flying Scotsman* emerges from under the beautiful roof of York station and comes to rest at platform 9A with the afternoon return working from Scarborough of the 'Scarborough Spa Express' on 25 May 1981.

This train was a forerunner of regular workings which ran on Tuesdays and Wednesdays from the middle of July to the end of August of that year using, as well as No. 4472, LNER A4 Pacific No. 4498 *Sir Nigel Gresley* and LMS Coronation Class 4–6–2 No. 46229 *Duchess of Hamilton*.

Introduction

Although steam returned to the main line on 2 October 1971 (after an absence of over three years) it would be fairly safe to say that it was towards the end of the 1970s, with the opening of more routes to steam power (notably the Settle & Carlisle line in 1978), that it became established. This was also due, in no small way, to the efforts of the Steam Locomotive Operators' Association (SLOA) under the able stewardship of Bernard Staite, who was the secretary of that esteemed association. SLOA was responsible not only for the marketing of many of the trains, but also had responsibility for the maintenance of the locomotives, making sure that they passed BR inspection in readiness for main line work.

For many, the 1980s were the zenith of main line steam specials, with not only an abundance of steam trains over the S&C line but also on the picturesque Fort William–Mallaig route, which began in 1984. If this were not enough for the enthusiast, the GWR 150-Year celebrations in 1985 saw the return of steam on many new routes, including the 'sea wall' between Exeter and Plymouth, bringing back many happy memories of holidays spent in South Devon to thousands of people (not least of all myself).

Add to all this the motive power to be seen over the decade from the diminutive North British 0–6–0 *Maude* to the LMS Coronation Pacific No. 46229 *Duchess of Hamilton*, and the BR infrastructures of the time such as signals and station areas, some of which have seen many changes, and it is easy to see why the decade is so popular in steam folklore and nostalgia.

In compiling this book, I am grateful for the help of many people, including all the photographers who contributed their valuable pictures: Hugh Ballantyne, David Eatwell, Keith Jackson, Pete Skelton, John Cooper-Smith, Robin Stewart-Smith. I would also like to thank my wife Christina who also typed the manuscript, and last but not least, all the railwaymen, amateur and professional alike, who make it possible for the rest of us to enjoy main line steam.

Note: Unless otherwise specified, all photographs were taken by the author.

Roger Siviter ARPS
Evesham, July 2003

Chapter One
Southern & South-West England

After a period of some twenty years, steam returned to the former Southern Railway Exeter route in October 1986. Early on the morning of Thursday 2 October 1986, ex-SR Bulleid 4–6–2 No. 35028 *Clan Line* was seen shunting stock at Salisbury station prior to leaving with a crew-familiarisation trip to Yeovil Junction and return. No. 35028 and support coach had arrived at Salisbury on the previous Monday (29 September) from Marylebone, running via Northolt Junction, Greenford, Reading, Swindon and Westbury.

Clan Line with the crew trip of 2 October is seen on the outward journey approaching Wilton junction (where the former GWR line to Westbury diverges). At the back of the train on this sunny but misty autumn morning can be seen the outline of Salisbury's famous medieval Cathedral, with its 400ft-high spire. Note also the allotments, a legacy of the Second World War.

Having been turned on Yeovil Junction's turntable, No. 35028 returned to Salisbury with its crew train, and is seen here passing through the now-closed station at Dinton (9 miles west of Salisbury) still with LSWR buildings. It is actually single line working here, the former Up line being used to provide a route to nearby military depots.

Some time later, *Clan Line*, having turned on the triangle to the east of Salisbury station, pauses in the elegant former LSWR station before being stabled in bay platform No. 5 prior to taking out the first public special train on the following Sunday (5 October).

Unlike 2 October, Sunday 5 October was a rather cloudy day. However, *Clan Line* complete with 'Atlantic Coast Express' (ACE) headboard looks a treat as it runs downgrade towards Tisbury with the morning return working from Yeovil Junction to Salisbury. The ACE was the crack train on this route, with many portions serving destinations in Devon and North Cornwall. It ran from 1926 to 1964, departing from Waterloo at 11.00 am.

The afternoon train on 5 October (the 1417 from Salisbury to Yeovil) was hauled by GWR modified Hall Class 4–6–0 No. 6998 *Burton Agnes Hall*. The train is seen here passing by the village of Tisbury on its journey to Yeovil Junction. No. 6998 was preserved by the Great Western Society and based at its Didcot Railway centre. The locomotive was one of a batch completed by Swindon works in January 1949 and bought in running order by the GWS in December 1965.

On the following Saturday (11 October 1986) there were two more return workings between Salisbury and Yeovil Junction. *Clan Line* with the morning return working from Yeovil is seen in sunny autumn weather as it emerges from Buckhorn Weston tunnel and heads down the 1 in 100 slope towards Gillingham and back to Salisbury. No. 35028 was built by the Southern Railway in 1948, rebuilt in 1959, and withdrawn from service in July 1967 with the end of steam on the Southern Region. It was then purchased from BR in running order by the Merchant Navy Locomotive Preservation Society and maintained in main line running order. At the time, it was based at Bulmers railway depot at Hereford.

In brilliant autumn sunshine (but characteristically with the exhaust clinging to the top of the boiler) *Clan Line* is seen in the Dorset countryside as it climbs the 1 in 100 gradient out of Gillingham towards Buckhorn Weston tunnel with the 1002 from Salisbury to Yeovil Junction on 11 October 1986.

More 'Blackmore Vale Express' trains were booked to run in 1988. On 30 June of that year ex-LMS Stanier Class 8F 2–8–0 No. 48151 is seen on a test run, heading out of Andover station towards Red Post junction, the junction for the freight-only branch line to Ludgershall. Some of the steam specials of that year traversed this branch, which originally ran through to Savernake. The 2–8–0 was a replacement for the Southern Railway King Arthur Class 4–6–0 No. 777 *Sir Lamiel*. This was perhaps one of the few occasions when an 8F 2–8–0 worked on this route. (*Hugh Ballantyne*)

Our next location is one of the most famous railway towns of all – Swindon. This Wiltshire town, located in the north of the county, was home to the giant GWR locomotive works, one of the most impressive workshops in the world. It was partly demolished in 1988 and the remains of it now form the GWR Railway Museum. However, in 1985 during the GWR 150-Year celebrations it was still in use. Here Castle Class No. 7029 *Clun Castle* stands outside the works on the evening of 27 August 1985, alongside a Class 08 diesel shunter, Class 47 No. 47484 and, round the corner, a Sultzer Class 25 diesel locomotive. The Castle had just worked in from Gloucester after a day's work on the Gloucester–Swindon trains, which ran during August of the GWR 150-Year celebrations.

Prior to the 1985 GWR celebrations, there were only spasmodic steam movements around the Bristol area. One of these took place on 2 June 1983 when GWR King Class 4–6–0 No. 6000 *King George V* (minus name-plates and commemorative bell) was seen climbing Ashley Hill bank in the northern suburbs of Bristol, heading towards Bristol Parkway and Swindon, with a running in turn from Swindon works, the outward journey being by Chippenham and Bath.

During the GWR 150-Year celebrations, special trains were run from Bristol Temple Meads to Portishead. On Sunday 21 July 1985, Class 2MT 2–6–0 No. 46443 (from the Severn Valley) ran under Brunel's famous Clifton Suspension Bridge in the Avon Gorge as it headed for Temple Meads with the day's first working from Portishead. This locomotive was built by BR at Crewe in 1950, and after withdrawal moved to the SVR in April 1967, being one of the first locomotives on the popular preserved line. (*David Eatwell*)

GWR locomotives King Class 4–6–0 No. 6000 *King George V* and Manor Class 4–6–0 No. 7819 *Hinton Manor* make a fine sight as they pull out of Bristol Temple Meads station on 7 April 1984 with a GWR 150 train to Plymouth, the 'Great Western Limited'. This was the first steam train to run on the main line in the West Country for over twenty years, but it proved an ill-fated trip, the King failing at Taunton and the Manor, with a pair of diesel Class 37s for part of the way, carrying on to Exeter, where it also failed. GWR Hall Class 4–6–0 No. 4930 *Hagley Hall* travelled overnight from the SVR at Bewdley to Plymouth, and on the following day (8 April) together with No. 7819 (which had been worked on through the night) the pair made the return trip from Plymouth to Bristol without a hitch, much to everyone's delight (see page 16). (*John Cooper-Smith*)

At around 8.00 pm on Sunday 8 September 1985 the light is fading fast as a Plymouth–Bristol special GWR 150 charter train speeds through the attractive GWR station at Yatton, some 12 miles south of Bristol on the line to Taunton. The crowds are out in force to see the special, which was hauled by Castle Class 4–6–0 locomotives No. 7029 *Clun Castle* and No. 5051 *Drysllwyn Castle*. *Clun Castle*, which was built in 1950, had a double chimney, and *Drysllwyn Castle*, built in 1936, had a single chimney. I mentioned that the light was fading, and I see from my records that even using 400 ASA film I was down to 125th second at f2.5!

On 14 July 1985, the Up 'Great Western Limited' is seen running eastwards out of Taunton on the four-track main line, which at the time ran as far as Cogload junction, some 5 miles from Taunton. The Taunton goods lines can be seen in the background, and at the rear of the train is Taunton East Junction signal-box. In charge of the special is No. 5051 *Drysllwyn Castle* and GWR Hall Class 4–6–0 No. 4930 *Hagley Hall*. On this occasion, because of difficulties with the late running of the Down train on the previous week (7 July) it was decided to run the train with two less coaches, and from Newton Abbot (instead of Plymouth) to Bristol.

The difficulties which the Down 'Great Western Limited' of 7 July experienced were on Dainton bank, which necessitated the train terminating at Totnes instead of Plymouth. This special is seen leaving Taunton with No. 5051 and No. 4930 in charge. Framing the train is a splendid GWR gantry signal. Note also the amount of trackwork.

By 1985, the West of England resignalling programme had started, but fortunately, apart from Exeter where the semaphores had been replaced by colour light signals in April of that year, most of the others survived 1985, and indeed, the Newton Abbot area semaphores and signal-boxes lasted until the end of April 1987.

I have previously mentioned the special of 7 April 1985 when the locomotives failed. This is the return working on the following day with No. 4930 *Hagley Hall* and No. 7819 *Hinton Manor* climbing the 1 in 115 gradient of Whiteball bank near Burlescombe with the Plymouth–Bristol special. Also, as a complete contrast with the previous day, we were blessed with spring sunshine.

Opposite: These next two views, taken at Tiverton Junction station on that very wet and fateful 7 April 1985, show *Hinton Manor* pausing to 'get its breath back' before heading for Exeter, albeit with the assistance of a pair of Class 37 diesel locomotives, Nos 37009 and 37178, at the rear of the train. They also show the lovely old GWR station signal-box and some of the semaphore signals that abounded in the area. However, with the Exeter resignalling scheme, they would become redundant by the following year, the signal-box being closed on 3 March 1986 and demolished on 30 March 1990.

The station itself closed on 9 May 1986, to be replaced by Tiverton Parkway station (a mile or so north of the old junction station) which was opened on 12 May 1986. Some of the junction station buildings and the platforms remained until the early 1990s when demolition took place.

The Up 'Great Western Limited' headed by Nos 5051 and 4930 runs along the causeway at Cockwood Harbour near Starcross, 14 July 1985. This location is more or less the start of the 'sea wall' section on the Exeter–Plymouth line, which is regarded by many people as one of the most scenic sections of line in the United Kingdom.

Beyond Cockwood, the line runs through Dawlish Warren and then past the south Devon seaside resort of Dawlish with its famous red cliffs. On 8 September, the Up 'Great Western Limited' hauled by a pair of GWR Castles Nos 7029 and 5051 heads out of Dawlish and past the red sandstone cliffs on its journey to Bristol.

After Dawlish, the line runs through a series of short tunnels at Coryton Cove and Horse Cove. This spectacular view was photographed on 14 July 1985 and shows the Up 'Great Western Limited' leaving Coryton tunnel and running past Coryton Cove. In charge are *Drysllwyn Castle* and *Hagley Hall*. (*Pete Skelton*)

At Teignmouth, the line turns inland and runs up the Teign Valley to Newton Abbot. *Hagley Hall* and *Hinton Manor* have passed through Teignmouth station and are starting the run on the coastal section with the Plymouth–Bristol train on 8 April 1985. *(John Cooper-Smith)*

The next location is Bishopsteignton in the Teign Valley, between Newton Abbot and Teignmouth. The date is 27 October 1985 and dusk is falling as *King George V* and *Hinton Manor* head eastwards with the final Up 'Great Western Limited' of the GWR 150-Year. It would be some years later, in 1994, before steam workings would return to this popular and photogenic main line.

No. 5051 looks a treat as it waits at the eastern end of Newton Abbot station (together with No. 4930 which is at the rear of No. 5051) to take out the Up 'Great Western Limited' of 14 July 1985. To complete this quintessential scene is part of the GWR gantry signal which controlled the Up main line of this South Devon junction station. No. 5051 was built by the GWR in 1936 and withdrawn from service in 1963. It was restored by the GWS at Didcot after rescue from Barry scrapyard in 1969.

Between Newton Abbot and Plymouth are the three notorious banks, Dainton, Rattery and Hemerdon. On 8 September 1985, Nos 5051 and 7029 start the climb of Dainton bank from the west with a Plymouth–Bristol special. Part of this climb is as steep as 1 in 38, and coming westwards it is even steeper in one place, at 1 in 36. (*John Cooper-Smith*)

Opposite, top: Crowds gather at the western end of Newton Abbot station as *Drysllwyn Castle* and *Hagley Hall* arrive with a Bristol to Plymouth special on 7 July 1985. In the background can be seen the diesel depot which was built on the site of the old steam shed 83A.

Opposite, bottom: The next scene shows the train in the previous picture departing from Newton Abbot for Plymouth. Note the signal-box and semaphore gantry signal and the building on the right-hand side now owned by the publishers David & Charles, but which was originally the wagon works. Within a mile of this location is Aller junction, where the line to Torquay and Paignton (and previously Kingswear) leaves the Plymouth line. (*Hugh Ballantyne*)

Just west of Totnes station is Rattery bank, with a gradient as steep as 1 in 46 for westbound (Down) trains. However, on this occasion (8 September 1985) Nos 5051 and 7029 *Dryslwyn Castle* and *Clun Castle* find the going easy as they speed downgrade into Totnes station with the Up 'Great Western Limited'.

To the east of Plymouth is Hemerdon bank, with one section for Up trains as steep as 1 in 42. On 1 September 1985, No. 5051 and No. 7029 top Hemerdon bank in fine style with a Plymouth–Bristol train. In the background are the fringes of Dartmoor National Park. This view clearly shows *Clun Castle*'s double chimney in contrast to the single chimney of No. 5051.

GWR King Class 4–6–0 No. 6000 *King George V* and GWR Manor Class 4–6–0 No. 7819 *Hinton Manor* are pictured at Plymouth Laira diesel depot, just prior to taking out the final Plymouth–Bristol train on 27 October 1985. No. 6000 was preserved by the National Railway Museum/Borough of Thamesdown, and at this time was on loan to H.P. Bulmer Ltd of Hereford. It is now preserved at Swindon Railway Museum. No. 7819 came from Barry scrapyard to the Severn Valley Railway in January 1973, and was preserved by the Hinton Manor Fund. Unlike No. 6000, which was withdrawn from BR in December 1962 after thirty-five years of service, No. 7819 was taken out of service in November 1965, having been built by the GWR in 1939.

On Friday 6 September 1985, steam returned to the Cornish main line for the first time since 1964. However, it was to be the only steam trip in Cornwall during the decade. The train, which was a return trip from Plymouth to Truro, was hauled by Tyseley stalwart GWR 4–6–0 *Clun Castle*. On the outward trip, the train stopped at Par, where No. 7029 was turned on the St Blazey shed (formerly 83E) turntable. It then took the train (running tender first) on the final 19 miles to Cornwall's only city.

This picture shows *Clun Castle* as it poses on the St Blazey turntable on that historic day. In the background are the shed buildings, home at the time to a small fleet of English Electric Class 37 diesel locomotives, which were mainly used on freight trains, particularly for the many china clay workings in the area. (*Pete Skelton*)

The next view shows the return working from Truro as it crosses over Coombe St Stephens viaduct, which is situated some 5 miles west of St Austell. Note the piers of the original Brunel timber viaduct on the left of the present one.

We complete this memorable day as *Clun Castle* crosses back into Devon via Brunel's magnificent Royal Albert Bridge. In the background is the Cornish border town of Saltash, which nestles on the banks of the River Tamar.

Chapter Two

The London Area
& the Home Counties

During the 1980s, the principal steam workings in the London area were the trains from Marylebone to Stratford-upon-Avon (and occasionally further afield) which commenced on 26 January 1985. However, odd workings did occur, for example Old Oak Common shed open day on 20 September 1981, when a shuttle service was run between Old Oak and Paddington, with GWR Castle Class 4–6–0 No. 5051 *Drysllwyn Castle* and BR 9F Class 2–10–0 No. 92220 *Evening Star* at either end.

Above is No. 5051 heading for Paddington, having just passed through Westbourne Park station. Note the London Transport lines in the foreground and the ubiquitous HST train in the background. (*Pete Skelton*)

Here is the 'other end' of the shuttle train (see page 27) at Royal Oak, with No. 92220 in charge as it heads for Old Oak Common. On the left-hand side can be seen part of the elevated A40(M) road. (*Keith Jackson*)

On 19 November 1984, A3 Pacific No. 4472 *Flying Scotsman* is seen near Canning Town with a gauging and route clearance test train, prior to working the Royal Train, which was to carry the Queen Mother from Stratford, east London, to North Woolwich the following day. (*Keith Jackson*)

Cannon Street station is our next unusual steam location. On 23 August 1986, SR King Arthur Class 4–6–0 No. 777 *Sir Lamiel* (now complete with smoke deflectors) is seen on exhibition at the former Southern Railway station, having moved from Marylebone via Neasden Junction from where it had a diesel pilot. Although the locomotive is in steam, the Southern Region at the time were adamant that steam would never run on third rail again, hence the sleepers and locks, ensuring that no movement would take place. (*Keith Jackson*)

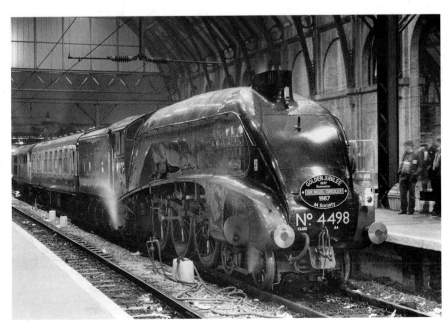

A4 Class Pacific No. 4498 *Sir Nigel Gresley* is seen at 0015 in the first hour of Sunday 31 May 1987, standing at platform 7 at London Kings Cross station. The locomotive was en route back to Marylebone after a visit to a Norwich Open Day. Since No. 4472 *Flying Scotsman* in 1969, this was the first appearance of a locomotive in steam at the 'Cross'. (*David Eatwell*)

Taken on 26 January 1985, LNER A4 4–6–2 No. 4498 *Sir Nigel Gresley* makes an impressive departure from the former Great Central Railway terminus at Marylebone. This train, the 'Thames–Avon Express' to Stratford-upon-Avon, was the first departure from the London terminus in the 1980s, thus starting a new era in main line steam running. Note the BR-style signal-box on the left-hand side. (*Keith Jackson*)

The Marylebone–Stratford-upon-Avon trains proved to be very popular and ran until 1990, when Marylebone station was refurbished. During that time, a wide variety of locomotives were used from the 'big four' companies and also BR Standard Class 4 4–6–0 No. 75069 from the Severn Valley Railway. It is seen here on Saturday 12 April 1986, waiting to leave the London terminus with the 'William Shakespeare' with which it ran through to Stratford-upon-Avon, unlike the Sunday trains, where steam would come off at Banbury and the trains would then go forward to Stratford hauled by diesel power. The steam locomotive would then work light to Hatton North junction and reverse down to Stratford in order to take the train back to London. (*Keith Jackson*)

A glorious sight at Marylebone on 31 August 1986, as ex-SR Pacific No. 35028 blasts out of the terminus with a heavy Pullman train bound for Stratford-upon-Avon. Note the 'Golden Arrow' regalia, and also the turntable on the right-hand side (see picture overleaf.) (*Keith Jackson*)

The turntable at Marylebone played a major part in the return to steam in London. Little work was needed to upgrade it for the extra axle weights of steam engines. It was still fully operational, being used for turning Class 115 DMU power cars as required. The turntable was removed a few years ago, and now resides at Fort William. On 18 May 1986, Castle Class 4–6–0 No. 7029 is being turned after working a route clearance special from Tyseley. No. 7029 was later to become a regular performer on the route, being based at Marylebone for a series of 'Shakespeare Limiteds'. (*Keith Jackson*)

For the first 2 miles out of Marylebone the line runs through three tunnels, the third of which is Hampstead tunnel, where the former GCR/LNER line crosses over the ex-LMS West Coast line out of Euston. On Sunday 11 May 1986, SR King Arthur Class 4–6–0 No. 777 *Sir Lamiel* heads out of Hampstead tunnel and crosses over the WCML with the 'Shakespeare Limited' to Stratford-upon-Avon. This veteran locomotive (the Class was introduced in 1925) was one of the most popular engines with the Marylebone footplate crews and performed many fine runs on the route, especially when smoke deflectors were fitted, as on this occasion. This was mainly because the locomotive had to be worked harder to lift the smoke from the driver's view.

At Hampstead tunnel again, this time showing No. 4472 *Flying Scotsman* on 26 October 1986. The author lived at West Hampstead in the late 1950s and 1960, and has many happy memories of Marylebone station and the GCR line which ran through West Hampstead. (*John Cooper-Smith*)

A famous visitor to the Marylebone line in 1986 was the world speed record holder LNER A4 Pacific No. 4468 *Mallard*, seen here at Neasden on 26 October 1986 with the second portion of the 'Shakespeare Limited' from Marylebone to Stratford-upon-Avon. The previous picture shows the first portion of this train which, due to its popularity, was often run in two sections. (*John Cooper-Smith*)

On 20 December 1986, Class N15 (King Arthur) 4–6–0 No. 777 *Sir Lamiel* runs through Northolt Junction with a Marylebone–High Wycombe 'Santa Steam Pullman'. This junction is where the GW/GC lines merge. The far side line is the Up line into Marylebone via Neasden Junction, with the other two being the Up and Down Paddington–Birmingham lines. (*Keith Jackson*)

Flying Scotsman approaches Northolt Junction on 3 January 1987 with a High Wycombe–Marylebone 'Santa Steam Pullman'. The train is about to pass under the famous splitting distant gantry, which has since been removed and is now fully restored and on display in the great hall at York Railway Museum. The exact location of this picture is Ruislip Gardens, about a mile north-west of Northolt Junction. (*Keith Jackson*)

No. 4498 *Sir Nigel Gresley* is framed by a fine array of GWR-style bracket signals as it approaches High Wycombe station with a South Ruislip to Stratford-upon-Avon special charter train, organised by the Cambridge University Railway Club, 11 May 1986.

Turning round from the picture on the previous page, we see GWR Castle Class 4–6–0 No. 7029 *Clun Castle* running through High Wycombe station on 23 May 1987 with a return Marylebone–Tyseley train. Note the GWR signal with route indicator and also the fine station canopy on the Up platform. The staggered Down platform is out of sight off the left-hand side. Also on the left can be seen part of the famous cutting wall, which contains around half a million bricks.

No. 777 runs through the cutting at the north end of High Wycombe station, passing the famous brick retaining wall. The train is a Marylebone–Stratford-upon-Avon 'Shakespeare Limited', seen on Sunday 11 May 1986.

Another route in the Home Counties that saw a fair amount of steam activity was that between Didcot, Oxford and Banbury (for Birmingham). The former GWR shed at Didcot is now the headquarters of the Great Western Society and is ideally placed to service steam locomotives, as well as being home to several locomotives used on the main line.

On this occasion, however, the steam locomotive was a visitor from another famous preserved locomotive depot – Tyseley. The pride of Tyseley, Castle Class 4–6–0 No. 7029 *Clun Castle*, is seen near Didcot North junction as it heads back to Birmingham late in the afternoon of 10 October 1981 with the 'Dinting Venturer'. This train originated in Manchester, and No. 7029 worked the Dorridge–Didcot–Dorridge section of the charter. In the background is the huge Didcot Power Station complex. (*Keith Jackson*)

Travelling north from Oxford, the line passes under the Paddington line at Aynho flyover, just under a mile south of Aynho junction, where the two lines converge. On 19 January 1980, GWR Castle Class 4–6–0 No. 5051 *Earl Bathurst* (later renamed *Drysllwyn Castle*) speeds under the flyover with a Didcot to Stratford-upon-Avon train composed of the Great Western Society's GWR coaching set. This together with the trip on the following Sunday (26 January) were to be the final runs with this beautiful coaching stock.

Another GWR Castle Class locomotive, this time 4–6–0 No. 5080 *Defiant*, which was preserved at Tyseley. No. 5080 approaches Aynho junction on 11 June 1988 with a Dorridge–Didcot charter train – 'The Red Dragon'. Note the mixture of upper and lower quadrant semaphore signalling, due to regional changes. Within a year or two of this picture being taken, colour lights would replace the semaphores. *Defiant* was another Barry scrapyard engine, and was originally purchased by the Standard Gauge Steam Trust at Tyseley for use as spare parts. It was built at Swindon in 1939 and originally named *Ogmore Castle*. The name was changed along with some other members of the Class in 1940/1. No. 5080 was withdrawn from service in April 1963.

A mile north of Aynho junction and 3 miles south of Banbury is the picturesque village of King's Sutton. For many years, this has been a popular location with railway photographers, especially for afternoon northbound trains. *Flying Scotsman* glows in the late autumn sunshine as it speeds towards Banbury with 'The Shakespeare Limited' from Marylebone to Stratford-upon-Avon on 2 November 1986.

On 27 May 1989, ex-LMS Jubilee Class 4–6–0 No. 45596 *Bahamas* made a welcome return to main line duty. It is seen here, resplendent in BR lined green livery, heading north at King's Sutton with a returning 'Derby Evening Telegraph' special from Derby to Didcot. In the background, obscured by exhaust in the previous picture, is the pinnacled spire of King's Sutton's fifteenth-century church.

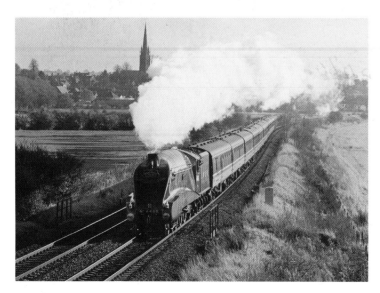

We finish this trio of pictures at King's Sutton with world record breaking A4 Pacific *Mallard* as it passes the outskirts of the medieval village with the second Marylebone–Stratford train on Sunday 2 November 1986. Both *Mallard* and *Flying Scotsman* (see opposite) will come off their trains at Banbury and work light to Stratford-upon-Avon.

We are now at Banbury station on Sunday 2 November 1986, where Nos 4468 and 4472, having come off their trains (these having worked forward to Stratford-upon-Avon by diesel power), are just leaving for Shakespeare's hometown in the heart of Warwickshire. This was truly an historic occasion for which, as you can see, the crowds had turned out to witness probably the two most famous steam locomotives in the world.

An earlier scene at Banbury station, 14 September 1980, with Castle Class No. 5051 waiting to leave with a special charter from Didcot to the Severn Valley Railway – 'The John Myners Memorial' train. The station buildings, although looking of very modern construction, date back to 1958. The previous station originally had an overall roof but this was removed in 1952.

On 19 January 1980, No. 5051 accelerates past the remains of Banbury goods yard and approaches the signal-box which controlled it. The train is the penultimate special from Didcot to Stratford-upon-Avon, which used the Great Western Society's GWR carriage set.

The following Sunday (26 January 1980) we see No. 5051 as it climbs Cropredy bank just north of Banbury with a Didcot to Stratford-upon-Avon special, the last time that the GWR coaches were used on the main line.

Chapter Three
The Midlands

This chapter begins in the East Midlands where, on 27 February 1983, steam returned to the East Coast Main Line when, appropriately, LNER A3 Class 4–6–2 No. 4472 *Flying Scotsman* hauled a special charter train from Peterborough to York. The train, which was formed of SLOA Pullman stock, originated at Kings Cross, from where it was hauled to Peterborough by Class 47 No. 47158 *Henry Ford*. No. 4472 is seen in its old stamping ground at Little Bytham in Lincolnshire, some 17 miles north of Peterborough. The train made stops at Newark and Doncaster before arriving at York.

During the spring and summer of 1989, several trains were run between Nottingham and Lincoln. They were known as 'The Lincolnshire Poacher'. On 3 June 1989, BR Standard Class 4 2–6–4T No. 80080 throws out a fine exhaust as it heads out of the Roman city of Lincoln for the medieval city of Nottingham. The location is at East Holmes, just west of Lincoln Central station. On the right-hand side are the remains of the old steam shed (40A).

No. 80080 was built by BR in 1954, withdrawn in 1965 and sent to Barry scrapyard, from where it was taken to the Peak Railway Society at Matlock for preservation. It is now based at the Midland Railway Centre at Butterley. (*Robin Stewart-Smith*)

Opposite: 'The Lincolnshire Poacher' bound for Nottingham makes a spirited departure from Lincoln Central station with ex-LMS 'Black Five' 4–6–0 No. 44932 in charge, 22 April 1989. This locomotive, after withdrawal from BR service, was preserved at the Greater Manchester Museum of Science and Technology, but like No. 80080 is now based at the Midland Railway Centre. (*Robin Stewart-Smith*)

Ex-LMS Jubilee Class 6P5F 4–6–0 No. 45596 *Bahamas* departs from Nottingham Midland station on the evening of 4 June 1989 and heads for the railway town (now city) of Derby with 'The Waverley' charter train. This handsome locomotive was one of only four of the Class to be fitted with a double chimney in its later BR days. It was also one of fifty locomotives to be built for the LMS by the North British Locomotive Co. in 1934/5. After withdrawal by BR in 1966, it was originally preserved by the Bahamas Locomotive Society at Dinting Railway Centre. (*John Cooper-Smith*)

The week commencing 1 June 1987 saw a series of daily special trains run between Dorridge and Wigston (Leicester), organised by Cromwell Engineering and called 'The Cromwell Pullman'. The first picture (opposite, bottom) shows *Flying Scotsman* and 'The Cromwell Pullman' heading for the Leicester area at Water Orton to the east of Birmingham. Water Orton is the junction for the Leicester and Derby routes, and the old signal-box (then a tool store and now demolished) was originally Water Orton East Junction signal-box.

The second picture (above) shows the ECS of the same special, having discharged its passengers at Wigston, heading up the Midland main line from Glen Parva North junction (where the line from Birmingham meets the St Pancras line) towards Leicester for stabling and engine turning.

The final scene (overleaf) shows No. 4472 and stock heading out of Leicester London Road station, bound for Wigston and then on to Dorridge. All three pictures were taken on Wednesday 3 June 1987. (*Third picture: John Cooper-Smith*)

We are now in the south Midlands and on the former GWR Paddington–Birmingham Snow Hill line. The location is Harbury cutting, 6 miles south of the Regency town of Royal Leamington Spa. On the evening of 27 July 1986, No. 777 hurries south with a return Stratford-upon-Avon–Marylebone train. Note the graceful brick-built farm bridge.

Southbound trains face a stiff 1 in 143 climb through Harbury cutting, but newly restored Jubilee 4–6–0 *Bahamas* seems to have plenty to spare as it heads towards Banbury with a Derby–Didcot special charter, 27 May 1989.

At Harbury cutting on 13 September 1981, BR Standard Class 9F 2–10–0 *Evening Star* catches the late afternoon sunlight with a return Stratford-upon-Avon–Didcot train – 'The Rising Star'. This location is just north of Harbury tunnel and some 14 miles north of Banbury.

Opposite: Unlike the East Midlands where, as has already been seen, steam charter trains were no more than sporadic throughout the 1980s, the south Midlands, notably the GWR line between Banbury and Birmingham/Stratford-upon-Avon, saw many trains throughout the decade. On this route, it would be fair to say that one of the most popular spots, both for watching and photographing northbound trains hard at work, is Hatton bank. This steep gradient starts just west of Warwick and runs for around 4 miles to Hatton Junction station. Almost throughout its length, grades vary between 1 in 87 and 1 in 110!

The first picture on Hatton bank was taken at the start of the climb, the 1 in 87/95 near Budbrooke. Castle Class No. 5051 *Drysllwyn Castle* is seen working very hard as it heads the northbound 'Devonian' on 9 October 1982. This train originated at Newton Abbot and was steam hauled from Didcot to Birmingham Moor Street, running outwards via Stratford-upon-Avon and the North Warwicks line, and returning via Dorridge.

No. 5051 again, this time at the head of a Didcot–Stratford-upon-Avon train as it climbs the 1 in 108 of Hatton bank just west of Budbrooke, Saturday 7 March 1987. On the left, through the trees, can just be glimpsed Hatton Hospital. Nearby Budbrooke church contains the grave of Field Marshal Lord Montgomery, Budbrooke barracks being for many years the regimental home of the Warwickshire Regiment – Monty's old regiment.

A sunnier day on Hatton bank, as Merchant Navy Pacific *Clan Line* glows in the spring sunshine as it heads for Stratford-upon-Avon with a train from Marylebone on Saturday 27 April 1985. The junction for the Stratford line (Hatton East junction) is just to the west of Hatton station. Hatton North junction (also for Stratford-upon-Avon) is ½ mile further on, thus forming a convenient triangle, ideal for turning steam locomotives.

Two months earlier the Hatton area was covered in snow, 18 February 1985. *Sir Nigel Gresley* complements this winter scene as it heads for Stratford-upon-Avon with the 'Thames–Avon Express' from Marylebone.

The northbound 'Dalesman' hauled by *Drysllwyn Castle* threads the attractive three-arch bridge, 1 mile east of Hatton station, on 9 May 1981. No. 5051 hauled the special from Didcot to Dorridge on the outward trip, and from Saltley to Didcot on the return. At this location, the line runs next to the Grand Union Canal, which it has roughly followed since leaving the county town of Warwick.

I mentioned earlier that Hatton bank was ideal for photographing westbound trains, but trains from Stratford-upon-Avon (as opposed to the Birmingham area) would need to work hard through Hatton East junction, and would often carry on doing so down the bank. This was certainly the case on Saturday 13 May 1989, as GWR 4–4–0 No. 3440 *City of Truro* and its InterCity liveried stock glow in the evening sunshine as they descend down to Warwick on a return BR special from Stratford to Didcot. This train was run to celebrate the return, in May 1989, of No. 3440 back into traffic, after being mainly on static display at the National Railway Museum at York since the GWR 150-Year celebrations of 1985.

Moving towards Birmingham on the GWR Banbury–Snow Hill line, we come to just north of Lapworth, which was originally a four-track section as far as Lapworth station. On 22 March 1986, BR Standard Class 4 4–6–0 No. 75069 heads towards Lapworth station with a York–Saltley–Didcot special. No. 75069 had come on the train at Saltley, the section from York having been worked by SR 4–6–0 No. 777 *Sir Lamiel* (see also pages 64 and 66). The four-track section between Tyseley and Lapworth was reduced to two tracks in about 1970.

Tyseley (junction for the North Warwicks line to Stratford-upon-Avon) is the next location as Gresley A3 Pacific No. 4472 *Flying Scotsman* heads for Solihull and Dorridge with a special train from Wigston near Leicester on the evening of Wednesday 3 June 1987 (see also pages 46, 47 and 48). At the rear of the train can be seen the junction for Stratford-upon-Avon and beyond that, Tyseley station building, which is roughly adjacent to the famous Tyseley Railway Museum.

During the 1980s, many trains ran to Stratford-upon-Avon, mainly from Didcot and Marylebone via Hatton East junction. However, on several occasions, Tyseley Museum would organise a day or a weekend of trips down the North Warwicks line to Stratford. One such day was Saturday 8 June 1985, when one of the Tyseley flagship locomotives 4–6–0 No. 7029 *Clun Castle* heads south near Earlswood with the 1248 Hall Green (Birmingham) to Stratford-upon-Avon train.

On a bright winter's afternoon on 26 January 1980 *Drysllwyn Castle* pulls out of Stratford-upon-Avon with a special charter returning to Didcot. Within a mile or so, it will begin to climb the 1 in 75 of Wilmcote bank, a stiff test for a heavily laden train. Just after Wilmcote is Bearley Junction, where the line to Hatton and Banbury leaves the North Warwicks line. Note also the semaphore signals, now long since gone. *(Christina Siviter)*

Opposite: Another day of steam trips took place on the North Warwicks line, on Saturday 7 June 1986. This time we see Tyseley's LMS Jubilee Class 4–6–0 No. 5593 *Kolhapur* with a Birmingham–Stratford-upon-Avon train between Earlswood and Wood End.

We leave the Birmingham area for the time being, and look at the specials trains that ran in Gloucestershire and Worcestershire during the 1980s. We begin in Gloucestershire, where steam returned during the GWR 150-Year celebrations, with a series of trains between Gloucester, Stroud and on to Swindon (see page 12). On 26 August 1985, No. 6000 *King George V* crosses Frampton Mansell viaduct (near Sapperton) some 6 miles east of the Cotswold town of Stroud, with the 1330 Gloucester–Swindon train, having earlier worked to Gloucester with the 1055 from Swindon. Up trains on the climb to Sapperton tunnel face gradients as steep as 1 in 60. In BR steam days, banking engines were used on this section, especially on the heavy coal trains and freight from South Wales and the Midlands. The banking engine which was shedded at Brimscombe (2 miles east of Stroud) was usually a GWR 2–6–2 tank.

Castle Class No. 5051 speeds through the attractive GWR station at Stroud on the morning of a very wet Thursday 15 August 1985. The train is the 1055 Swindon to Gloucester.

King George V and a smart rake of maroon coaches run down grade towards Standish junction with the return 'Severn–Wye Express' from Swindon to Hereford via Gloucester and Newport on Saturday 9 May 1987. This location is halfway between Stroud and Gloucester (10 miles in total). The tracks in the foreground are the Midland main line from Bristol to Birmingham, which connect with the GWR Gloucester to Swindon line at Standish junction.

Turning round from the picture above, we see the Bristol and Swindon lines as they start to merge, the actual Standish junction is out of sight on the top left-hand side. Standard Class 4MT 4–6–0 No. 75069 catches the late evening sun as it climbs the 1 in 347 towards Stonehouse and Stroud with the 1855 Gloucester–Swindon train on 20 August 1985. The GWR chocolate and cream carriages all add to the scene.

On Sunday 25 August 1985, No. 7029 *Clun Castle* draws into the platform at Gloucester station with the 1055 train from Swindon. On the left-hand side of the picture can be seen the spire of St Peter's church. The lines straight ahead are to Chepstow and Newport. The cross-country trains between the South-West and the Midlands (and the north of England) reverse at the station. There is also an avoiding line to the east of the station for the non-stop Bristol and Birmingham trains.

By courtesy of BR, the photographer was able to take a dramatic night picture of the mighty *King George V* resting over the inspection pits at Gloucester maintenance depot, after working on the Gloucester/ Swindon trains on 26 August 1985. Note the shed plate – 85C – Gloucester Barnwood shed. (*Pete Skelton*)

GWR Castle Class 4–6–0 No. 5051 *Defiant* is seen near Churchdown on what used to be the GWR/LMS four-track section between Cheltenham and Gloucester, 6 August 1988. The train is 'The Red Dragon' from Worcester to Newport.

Still on the Birmingham–Bristol main line, this time in the beautiful Worcestershire countryside near Defford, just south of Worcester in the Vale of Evesham, 3 September 1985. GWR 4–4–0 No. 3440 *City of Truro* and Collett brake composite No. 6913 make steady progress with a Gloucester to Worcester and Kidderminster (SVR) trial run. In the background, the western slopes of Bredon Hill, rising to around 900 feet, are a prominent feature.

The outward journey from Kidderminster to Gloucester of No. 3440 on its trial trip, 3 September 1985. The location is Norton Junction (Worcester) where the Oxford and Paddington line leaves the line to Gloucester. There was a small halt here (I know – I used it in my Army days!) for the nearby Norton barracks, but there seems very little evidence of it now.

During the 1980s, the line from Hereford to Worcester saw only sporadic steam working, comprising locomotive positioning runs to and from the SVR for work on the Welsh Marches route, and also the occasional charter train, as on Sunday 12 June 1983, when LMS Class 5 4–6–0 No. 5000 is caught by the camera as it crosses the River Severn and runs into Worcester with a train from Hereford and Newport. The section from Bristol to Newport had been worked by GWR 4–6–0 *King George V* (see page 72). At the time No. 5000, which had been preserved by the National Railway Museum at York, was on loan to the Severn Valley Railway. (*David Eatwell*)

The Worcester, Kidderminster, Stourbridge Junction and Birmingham line at Rainbow Hill tunnel can be seen, just to the north of Worcester Shrub Hill station. On the evening of Friday 12 September 1986, Class 2F 0–6–2 tank LNWR No. 1054 (BR No. 58926) emerges from Rainbow Hill tunnel and passes a fine-looking GWR bracket signal as it heads for Kidderminster and the Severn Valley Railway. It had come from Dinting Railway Centre via Chester and Hereford. This Class of locomotives, known as 'Coal Tanks', were designed by Webb for the LNWR and introduced in 1882. During September, the pre-grouping locomotive would be an attractive feature on the SVR and would return to its home base on 18 October with the SLS/W. A. Camwell special train (see also page 86).

It is 9.00 pm on the evening of Saturday 26 June 1986, and No. 7029 *Clun Castle* propels its support coach across Kidderminster viaduct and heads for Droitwich where it will reverse and take the line through Bromsgrove and up the Lickey bank to its home base of Tyseley. The locomotive had spent the previous week working on the SVR. In the 1980s, apart from these locomotive movements, it was rare to see steam on this route.

Leaving Worcestershire, we return to the Birmingham area where, on 5 October 1985, ex-LMS Coronation Pacific No. 46229 *Duchess of Hamilton* heads eastwards towards Water Orton where it will take the Derby line with 'The South Yorkshireman' train from London Marylebone to Sheffield Midland station.

The location is Bromford Bridge, some 3 miles from the centre of Birmingham. On the right-hand side is part of the elevated section of the M6 motorway, overlooked by the cooling towers of Nechells power station, and on the left-hand side is Saltley gasworks. The power station has since been demolished, but the gas holders still remain. At the rear of the train are Washwood Heath sidings and yard.

On 22 March 1986 Maunsell Class N15 4–6–0 No. 777 *Sir Lamiel* (minus smoke deflectors) heads south at Wychnor junction near Alrewas (Staffordshire) with 'The South Yorkshireman' from York to Saltley and Didcot, the Saltley to Didcot section being worked by 4–6–0 No. 75069 (see page 54).

Tyseley's Jubilee Class 4–6–0 No. 5593 *Kolhapur* heads out of Milford tunnel, just to the north of Derby on the line to Chesterfield, with 'The Lancashire Coast Express' from Derby to Southport via the Hope Valley route through Chinley on 25 August 1986. (*John Cooper-Smith*)

Just north of Belper on the Derby–Chesterfield/Sheffield line is Ambergate, junction for the former Midland line to Manchester via Millersdale and Chinley, which is now truncated at Matlock. This elevated junction also had a line at its northern end connecting the Sheffield and Manchester lines and thus forming a triangle. No. 777 heads south through the junction on 22 March 1986 with a train from York to Didcot. The old Manchester route, now a single line branch to Matlock, can be seen swinging away to the left.

In the summer of 1987, a series of trains were run from Nottingham to Matlock via Derby; these were known as 'The Derwent Explorer'. In pouring midsummer rain, ex-Somerset & Dorset Class 7F 2–8–0 No. 53809 passes through Cromford station on the Matlock branch with the northbound train on 19 July 1987. No. 53809 was shedded at the Midland Railway Centre at Butterley, where it had been privately preserved. (*Hugh Ballantyne*)

Ten miles north of Ambergate and 5 miles south of Chesterfield is Clay Cross junction, where the lines from Derby and Nottingham meet. At Tupton, just north of the junction, ex-SR unrebuilt Bulleid West Country Class Pacific No. 34092 *City of Wells* speeds south with a Sheffield to Marylebone train on 21 May 1988. These attractive lightweight 4–6–2s were first introduced in 1945 for use primarily on the SR's West of England lines.

The Hope Valley route is at the northern end of the Derbyshire Peak District. In the 1980s this line from Sheffield to Manchester saw fewer trains than the Derby–Sheffield line. However, on 26 April 1986 LNER Class V2 2–6–2 No. 4771 *Green Arrow* travelled over this attractive route with a twelve-coach York–Manchester charter train. The special is seen near Edale heading for Manchester. The V2 2–6–2s were designed by Sir Nigel Gresley and introduced in 1936. They were very powerful locomotives, and during the Second World War were renowned for hauling twenty-coach trains on the ECML between Kings Cross, York and Newcastle.

Just to the east of Chinley on the Hope Valley line is the triangular junction for the freight-only line to Peak Forest and around to Buxton. On 24 October 1987, ex-LMS Class 8F No. 48151 – newly restored by the Midland Railway Trust at Butterley – is seen en route for Peak Forest crossing the imposing viaduct which makes one third of the triangular junction, from Chinley East to Chinley South junction. The train had originated at Derby. (*Hugh Ballantyne*)

The same train as on the previous page, only this time threading the impressive rock cutting just south of Dove Holes tunnel (about a mile north of Peak Forest). This section of line from Chinley junction is the remaining northern end of the Derby–Manchester LMS (Midland) line. (*John Cooper-Smith*)

Chapter Four
Wales & the Borders

During the GWR 150-Year celebrations of 1985, apart from the South-West, another area that saw steam working for the first time in over twenty years was West Wales, namely the Swansea–Carmarthen line (it was 1992 before steam ran through to Tenby and Fishguard). The workings occurred over the weekend of 21/22 September, with GWR Modified Hall Class 4–6–0 No. 6960 *Raveningham Hall* in charge.

There were three workings each way between Swansea and Carmarthen, and No. 6960 is seen with the first return working of Saturday 21 September, the 1030 Carmarthen–Swansea. The location is St Ishmael, between Ferryside and Kidwelly, where the line skirts Carmarthen Bay. Note the 'Pembroke Coast Express' headboard.

Apart from seeing and travelling on steam on new routes, 1985 also saw the appearance of 'new' locomotives on special charters. For many people, one of the highlights of the GWR 150-Year was the sight of the Severn Valley Railway's GWR Churchward Class 28xx 2–8–0 No. 2857 on a special freight train at Newport on 10 September 1985. No. 2857 had run overnight from Kidderminster (SVR) to Newport with a rake of mixed vans and wagons, and while at Newport performed a special run-past from Alexandra Docks goods yard to Newport station (and on to the Usk river bridge). The first picture shows the veteran 2–8–0 as it heads tender-first towards Hillfield (Newport) tunnel en route to Newport Alexandra Docks goods yard, and the second shows it leaving the goods yard a short while later with the demonstration freight train.

Also on the same day Castle Class 4–6–0 No. 7029 *Clun Castle* worked into Newport from Gloucester with a special 'Pullman' charter train. After a lengthy break, the train returned to Gloucester, and is seen here in lovely late summer sunshine as it sets out from Newport and crosses the Usk river bridge en route to the cathedral city. This train together with No. 2857 and the beautiful late summer weather combined to make this a very memorable day indeed.

Just after the line crosses the River Usk, it comes to the junction for the North & West line to Hereford and Shrewsbury, but for the time being we remain on the South Wales/Paddington line, and also have a look at the line to Gloucester, which leaves the Paddington line at Severn Tunnel Junction. There can be very few finer sights than a top-class express locomotive at speed on a four-track main line. Hauling ten attractive maroon coaches GWR King Class 4–6–0 No. 6000 *King George V* is caught by the camera as it hurries along the South Wales to Paddington main line with a Hereford, Newport and Swindon charter train on 9 May 1987. The location is Magor, situated some 7 miles east of Newport and 2 miles west of the Severn Tunnel Junction.

On 12 June 1983, *King George V* runs through the Severn Tunnel Junction station towards Newport with 'The Brunel Pullman' train from Bristol. This was organised in connection with the Brunel Engineering Centre Trust celebrations at Bristol. After a stop at Newport for turning, the train ran to Hereford, where LMS Class 5 4–6–0 No. 5000 hauled the train to Worcester. The final section back to Bristol was hauled by Class 47 diesel No. 47500 *Great Western*.

Just east of Severn Tunnel Junction station the line to Gloucester leaves the South Wales–Paddington line, running through the riverside town of Chepstow where, on the evening of 10 September 1985, GWR 2–8–0 No. 2857 is seen heading back to the Severn Valley Railway with the charter freight train (see page 70). The GWR station and splendid footbridge complete this almost timeless scene. (*Hugh Ballantyne*)

Another fine locomotive that ran on the main line during the GWR 150-Year celebrations was GWR City Class 4–4–0 No. 3440 *City of Truro*, the first locomotive reputed to have reached the magic three-figure speed – 102.3 mph down Whiteball bank on 9 May 1904 with a Plymouth–Paddington 'Ocean Mail Express'.
The veteran locomotive runs out of Newnham tunnel (a few miles south-west of Gloucester) with a Gloucester–Newport special, on Sunday 20 October 1985. (*John Cooper-Smith*)

We leave the Newport–Gloucester line and travel on the North & West route, which follows the Welsh/English border closely from Newport to Chester, calling at Hereford and Shrewsbury (for Crewe) among the many medieval border towns on this route. This area is known as the Welsh Marches, and is steeped in history, with many fine castles still remaining. GWR Hall Class 4–6–0 No. 4930 *Hagley Hall* and Castle Class 4–6–0 No. 7029 *Clun Castle* leave the Welsh market town of Abergavenny behind as they hurry down the 1 in 153 gradient towards Newport with a Kidderminster, Hereford and Cardiff charter train on 6 July 1985. Once again, this was one of the many trains run to celebrate the GWR 150-Year celebrations.

From the return of steam on 2 October 1971, when No. 6000 *King George V* pulled out of a misty Hereford with the Bulmer's Pullman train, the Welsh Marches route has seen a great deal of activity, especially in the early to mid-1980s, with the 'Welsh Marches Pullman' and the 'Welsh Marches Express' trains being run on a semi-regular basis. Over that period of time, many locomotives were in charge of these popular trains. A fairly rare combination of motive power was to be seen on 26 February 1983, when BR Standard Class 4MT 2–6–4 tank No. 80079 and ex-LMS Class 4MT 2–6–0 No. 43106 (both from the Severn Valley Railway) worked the northbound WMP from Newport to Shrewsbury. The pair are seen just south of Abergavenny with the eleven-coach load.

Some 10 miles north of Abergavenny, southbound trains face the stiff climb to Llanvihangel summit, which is around 6 miles with a 1 in 99 grade at its steepest. On 11 April 1981, LMS Pacific No. 6201 *Princess Elizabeth* starts the climb of Llanvihangel bank with a southbound 'Welsh Marches Express'.

The three pictures on this page were taken on 24 May 1986, when my wife Christina and I travelled on a special over the Welsh Marches, first from Hereford to Shrewsbury and then back to Hereford, and then on to Newport. Motive power for the Hereford–Shrewsbury–Hereford section was provided by GWR 4–4–0 *City of Truro* and GWR 4–6–0 *King George V*, and GWR 4–6–0 *Clun Castle* for the Hereford–Newport leg. Nos 3440 and 6000 are seen running through Hereford station in order to join the special which had just arrived from Birmingham New Street.

The northbound special, just south of Ludlow tunnel. These two locomotives make a classic GWR scene, very reminiscent of when GWR 4–4–0s piloted trains from Newton Abbot over the South Devon banks, especially when they had thirteen coaches on, as was the case on this occasion. (*David Eatwell*)

The final scene in this trio of pictures shows the special on its return to Hereford station with No. 7029 waiting to take charge for the run to Newport. On that run, someone in our carriage who was timing the train reckoned that *Clun Castle* reached over 80 mph down Llanvihangel bank. A fitting end for a very enjoyable trip! (For a picture of this train at Shrewsbury, see page 81.)

During the 1980s, the Welsh Marches route certainly saw a wide variety of mainly large locomotives. On 20 May 1989, newly restored to main line running, ex-SR West Country Pacific No. 34027 *Taw Valley* hurries through Woofferton (formerly the junction for the line to Tenbury Wells and Kidderminster) with 'The West Mercian' from Crewe to Hereford.

LMS Princess Royal Class 4–6–2 No. 6201 *Princess Elizabeth* first ran on the line on 24 April 1976, which in fact was its first main line run, and was a fairly regular performer on the route during the 1980s. It is seen here approaching Craven Arms station on 7 March 1981 with a southbound 'Welsh Marches Express'. Just south of the station is the junction for the Central Wales line to Swansea.

The very last steam locomotive built by British Railways was Standard Class 9F 2–10–0 No. 92220 *Evening Star*, which was built at Swindon Works in March 1960. It was withdrawn in March 1965 and preserved at the National Railway Museum at York, which then loaned it to the Great Western Society at Didcot. It resumed main line running in 1981, and appeared on the North West route in 1983, when this picture of it was taken, leaving Craven Arms with a northbound WMP on 21 May of that year.

One of the great events of the 1980s was the return to main line running of Sir William Stanier's magnificent LMS Coronation Class Pacific No. 46229 *Duchess of Hamilton* in May 1980. It visited the Welsh Marches route in the autumn of 1982, and on 6 November of that year was photographed heading north out of Craven Arms with a 'Welsh Marches Express'.

A wintry scene, caused by a late fall of snow on 25 April 1981, as *King George V* heads north out of Church Stretton with a Hereford to Chester special charter train.

We now leave the Welsh Marches line for the time being, and go west of Shrewsbury to the Cambrian lines between Machynlleth and Barmouth/Aberystwyth where, in the summer of 1987, steam returned for the first time in twenty years. The first picture shows a scene reminiscent of BR steam days, as GWR Manor Class 4–6–0 No. 7819 *Hinton Manor* and ex-LMS Class 2MT 2–6–0 No. 46443 (both from the Severn Valley Railway) pose outside the old steam shed at Machynlleth (89C) on the evening of 2 August 1987. (*Hugh Ballantyne*)

On the morning of 26 May 1987, *Hinton Manor*, in lined black livery, looks a treat as it coasts into Dovey Junction with the 0940 Machynlleth to Barmouth train – 'The Cardigan Bay Express'. To complete this GWR scene is the rake of chocolate and cream coaching stock, and GWR bracket signals.

No. 7819 once again, this time in the Aberystwyth platform at Dovey Junction, just about to leave with the afternoon Machynlleth to Aberystwyth train, 2 August 1987. All the semaphore signals at this junction station have long since been replaced by colour light signalling. (*Hugh Ballantyne*)

GWR 4–4–0 No. 3440 and 4–6–0 No. 6000 receive admiring glances prior to leaving Shrewsbury with a special train to Hereford and Newport, 24 May 1986 (see also page 75).

Opposite, top: The highlight of the run by train from Machynlleth to Barmouth must be travelling over the famous Barmouth bridge, which crosses the Mawddach estuary. No. 7819 *Hinton Manor* heads off the bridge with the 1445 from Machynlleth on a sunny 24 May 1987. As in the early 1980s, there are now weight restrictions on the bridge, allowing only units to traverse it. These were reimposed in the early 1990s. However, steam excursions still run to Towyn, some 12 miles south of Barmouth. (*John Cooper-Smith*)

Opposite, bottom: We are now back on the Welsh Marches route at Sutton Bridge junction, Shrewsbury. This is the junction for the Cambrian line, and was also the junction for the Severn Valley line to Bridgnorth and Hartlebury (for Worcester). The remains of this line (although truncated a few feet on) can be seen in the centre foreground. On 26 August 1989, ex-SR Merchant Navy Pacific No. 35028 *Clan Line* eases round the curves at Sutton Bridge with a Shrewsbury, Newport, Gloucester and Swindon charter train. In the background is the medieval Shrewsbury Abbey.

Severn Valley locomotives ex-LMS Class 4MT 2–6–0 No. 43106 and GWR Manor Class 4–6–0 No. 7812 *Erlestoke Manor* climb the 1 in 165 gradient near Leaton, some 4 miles north of Shrewsbury, with a Chester-bound Welsh Marches Pullman on 5 June 1982. No. 43106 was one of the last of its class to work on BR, being withdrawn on 23 June 1968 from Lostock Hall shed, Preston. It was then bought by eighteen members of the SVR and ran in steam to the SVR at Bridgnorth in August 1968. No. 7812 was withdrawn from service in November 1965 and lay in Barry scrapyard for several years, from where it was rescued by the Erlestoke Manor Fund. It moved to the Severn Valley Railway in April 1976. (*Pete Skelton*)

On the line between Shrewsbury and Chester are two splendid viaducts. The first of these is the Chirk viaduct, situated some 3 miles north of Gobowen on the Shropshire/Wales border. This viaduct runs parallel with the aqueduct which carries the Shropshire Union Canal. The aqueduct can be seen in this view, as Southern Railway Lord Nelson Class 4–6–0 No. 850 *Lord Nelson* runs over Chirk viaduct with a Chester-bound special, 13 June 1981.

The other impressive viaduct is the Pentre, or Dee, viaduct, 3 miles south of Ruabon. It is 1,508 feet long, 147 feet high and has nineteen arches. Welsh Marches favourite No. 6201 *Princess Elizabeth* is seen crossing this elegant structure on 11 April 1987 with a York–Chester–Shrewsbury train, appropriately called 'The White Rose'.

For the first time since 1966, steam returned on the North Wales route between Crewe, Chester and Holyhead at the end of the decade in the summer of 1989. On 23 July 1989, rebuilt West Country Pacific No. 34027 *Taw Valley* passes by the thirteenth-century Conway Castle as it emerges from Robert Stephenson's tubular bridge with 'The North Wales Express' from Crewe to Holyhead. (*Hugh Ballantyne*)

Stanier Pacific No. 6201 *Princess Elizabeth* skirts the North Wales coast as it runs through Penmaenmawr with a Crewe–Holyhead 'North Wales Coast Express' on 3 September 1989. In the background is part of the Great Orme headland, which is just to the north-west of the famous seaside resort of Llandudno. (*Hugh Ballantyne*)

We leave the North Wales line and return to the Welsh Marches route where it enters the ancient Roman city of Chester. 'The White Rose' (see page 83) heads south out of Chester across the River Dee on 11 April 1987. In the background is part of the famous racecourse, known as The Roodee. At one time this was a four-track section as far as Saltney (junction for the North Wales route) about a mile south of here, but two tracks were taken up in about 1980.

After crossing the River Dee, the line then crosses over the Shropshire Union Canal at Northgate lock. No. 6201 with a special memorial train to Jack Street (from Crewe to Holyhead) crosses over the canal, 10 September 1989. The lock gates can be seen on the right-hand side.
(*Hugh Ballantyne*)

On 18 October 1986, a Stephenson Locomotive Society steam special was run from Shrewsbury to Stockport to celebrate the eightieth birthday of the famous railway historian and photographer, W.A. ('Cam') Camwell. It was hauled by LNWR Webb 0–6–2T coal tank No. 1054. The special train is seen here leaving Chester for Stockport on the final leg of that famous trip.

Chapter Five
The North-West

Where better to start this north-western chapter than at the famous railway town of Crewe, in the heart of Cheshire. On 20 June 1989, ex-SR West Country Pacific No. 34027 *Taw Valley* pulls out of the old LNWR/LMS station at Crewe and heads for Chester on the first leg of the 'press run' to Holyhead of the 'North Wales Coast Express'. (*Hugh Ballantyne*)

The attractive station at Northwich on the former Cheshire Lines Committee (CLC) line from Chester to Stockport is the setting as SR 4–6–0 No. 777 rolls in with a Hull, Leeds, Chester train on Saturday 5 March 1983 – 'The Deeside Venturer'. After arrival at Chester, *Sir Lamiel* was scheduled to haul the Chester to Shrewsbury section of 'The Welsh Marches Pullman' train. (*Pete Skelton*)

We are still on the CLC line to Stockport, this time at Knutsford where, on 21 June 1980, ex-SR Merchant Navy 4–6–2 No. 35028 *Clan Line* runs through the station with a Liverpool, Guide Bridge, Chester and Hereford train. This train was billed as 'The Clan Line Farewell', the locomotive remaining at Hereford for retubing and general repair. Note the interesting architecture of the waiting room on the right-hand side and also the platform canopy. Overlooking the scene is the medieval parish church.

In the 1980s, Manchester Victoria station was often the starting and finishing point for many steam specials. Over the decade, this former Lancashire & Yorkshire Railway (L&YR) station saw many different locomotives, including the former LNWR 0–6–2 coal tank No. 1054. On 27 June 1984, No. 1054 and a directors' saloon coach ran a series of shuttle trains between Manchester Victoria and Wilson's Brewery sidings near Newton Heath. The 'Wilson Brewery Special', headed by the handsome coal tank, is seen leaving Victoria station and heading for Newton Heath. Today, where the roof of the station had been is now a shopping complex.

This classic scene at Manchester Victoria was taken on 15 October 1988, but reminds me very much of when I used to visit the station in BR times between 1966 and 1968. Ex-LMS 'Black Five' 4–6–0 No. 44932 is in just the right position for the camera as it waits to return to Derby with 'The Mancunian'. These ubiquitous 4–6–0s were designed for the LMS by Sir William Stanier and introduced in 1934. They were equally at home on freight or passenger workings, and had the distinction of hauling the very last BR steam train on 11 August 1968. (*Robin Stewart-Smith*)

During the summer of 1980, BR ran a series of weekly specials between Manchester and Liverpool as part of the 'Rocket 150' celebrations. On 6 July 1980, LMS Jubilee Class 4–6–0 No. 5690, having just left Manchester Victoria station, pulls through the disused Manchester Exchange station. The two stations were connected, the connecting platform being the longest in the country at 2,194 feet – this consisted of Victoria's platform No. 11 and Exchange's platform No. 3. Exchange station was built by the LNWR in 1884, some forty years after Victoria station. Originally, the LNWR had shared Victoria station with the L&YR until Exchange was opened. Exchange station was closed in 1969 and all its passenger services rerouted into Victoria. (*John Cooper-Smith*)

Another 'Rocket 150' Manchester–Liverpool train, this time on Sunday 29 June 1980. LMS 4–6–2 No. 6201 *Princess Elizabeth* speeds through Eccles on its 31¾-mile journey to Liverpool, much to the enjoyment of the many onlookers.

Remaining on the old LNWR Manchester–Liverpool route, this time at the historic location of Rainhill, where around 1830 the famous locomotive trials took place. On 11 March 1981, SR Lord Nelson Class 4–6–0 No. 850 *Lord Nelson* comes under the skew bridge at the western end of Rainhill station and heads for Manchester and York with a special train from Liverpool Lime Street to commemorate the 150th anniversary of troop-carrying trains.

Recently overhauled 'Black Five' 4–6–0 No. 44932 pulls out of Southport with the 0930 to Wigan on Sunday 3 November 1985. This was the first of four return special trains between Southport and Wigan that day. Note the locomotives shed code – 11A (Carnforth). (*David Eatwell*)

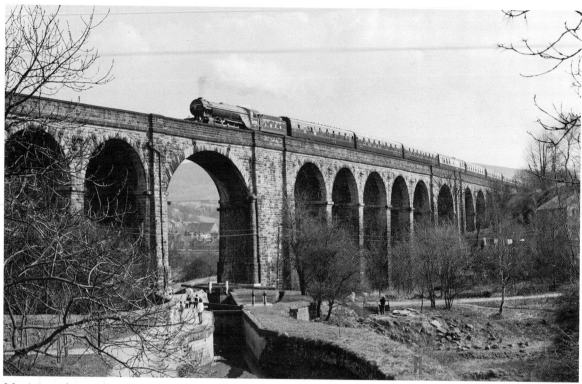

Moving to the north-east of Manchester, we come to the Manchester–Huddersfield line (via Stalybridge) – the Diggle route. This Pennine route saw quite a few steam excursions throughout the 1980s, including this one on 26 April 1986, when LNER V2 Class 2–6–2 No. 4771 *Green Arrow* is seen heading over the graceful Saddleworth viaduct with a Manchester–York train. At this point, the line is crossing over the Huddersfield & Ashton Canal. No. 4771 is preserved at the National Railway Museum at York.

During 1981 and 1982, a series of charter trains were run called 'The Trans Pennine Pullman'. The route for these trains was either Northwich, Leeds and Carnforth on the northbound workings or the reverse for the southbound trains. On 10 April 1982, Jubilee 4–6–0 No. 5690 *Leander* climbs the 1 in 175 gradient up Diggle bank near Saddleworth with the northbound 'Trans Pennine Pullman'. This was to be the final run of this particular train.

With a clear road ahead, *Lord Nelson* climbs the final mile at 1 in 125 gradient up to Diggle summit with the '150th Anniversary Troops By Train' special on 11 March 1981 (see also picture on page 91). Once it reaches the summit, the train will run on the level through the 3½ miles of Standedge tunnel. On emerging from this lengthy tunnel, the train finds the next 6 miles to Huddersfield through Slaithwaite and Golcar are downhill, giving the crew a welcome breather. These powerful 4–6–0 locomotives were designed by Maunsell for the Southern Railway, and introduced in 1926. They were modified by Bulleid in 1938. No. 850 was the only member of the Class to survive, being preserved by the National Railway Museum at York. At this time, it was on loan to Carnforth.

We are now back on the northern outskirts of Manchester at Miles Platting Junction. This location is the junction for Stalybridge to the east, and Rochdale and Todmorden to the north. Class 5MT 4–6–0 No. 44932 approaches the junction with a return Manchester Victoria–Derby train ('The Mancunian') on 15 October 1988. This train will run for around a mile on the Stalybridge line (left foreground) and then swing southwards at Park junction and head for Derby via Marple and the Hope Valley line. (*John Cooper-Smith*)

A rare occurrence on Wednesday 28 September 1983 as Midland 'Compound' Class 4P 4–4–0 No. 1000 leaves Winterbutlee tunnel near Walsden on the Todmorden–Manchester line with a York–Rochdale BR private charter train, which ran via Micklefield, Leeds and the Calder Valley route. The 'Compound' was the first steam locomotive to work over the L&YR Calder Valley main line since *Flying Scotsman* on 7 May 1969.

On 23 February 1985, the 'Thames–Eden Express' from London to Carlisle was steam-hauled from Manchester Victoria to Carlisle, via Blackburn and the Settle & Carlisle line. The special, hauled by 'Black Five' 4–6–0 No. 44767 and Jubilee 4–6–0 No. 5690 *Leander*, was photographed just south of Bolton station on its journey to Blackburn and Carlisle. (*Hugh Ballantyne*)

After Bolton, the line to Blackburn crosses over the attractive Entwistle viaduct, situated between Entwistle and Darwen, where on the evening of 3 May 1980 LNER A4 Pacific No. 4498 *Sir Nigel Gresley* catches the late evening sun as it hurries south with a Carnforth–Manchester Victoria special. (*Pete Skelton*)

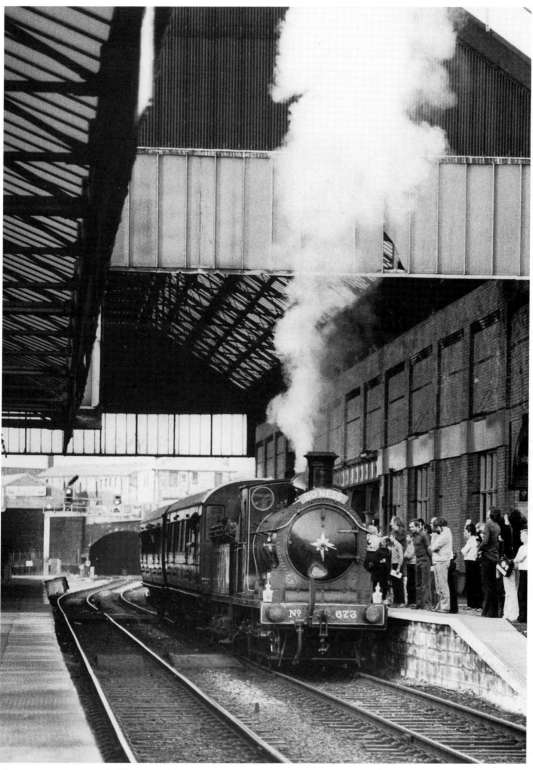

As part of the 'Rainhill 150' celebrations (to commemorate the Rainhill trials of 1830) locomotives came from far and wide. One such engine was former LNER Class J36 0–6–0 No. 673 (BR No. 65243) *Maude*, seen here after arrival at Blackburn station en route to Manchester (for Rainhill) on the evening of Saturday 17 May 1980. The locomotive and two coaches had travelled from its base at the Scottish Railway Preservation Society at Falkirk via the Glasgow and South Western route and the Settle & Carlisle line, quite a journey for a locomotive built in 1888! The station at this famous north Lancashire town has since been modernised and the roof has now been removed.

No. 673 is seen on its epic journey of 17 May 1980 north of Blackburn near Clitheroe on the line from Hellifield Junction. This was the longest journey to be undertaken by any steam locomotive coming to the 'Rainhill 150' celebrations. Note also the Caledonian Railway coaches.

LNER Pacific No. 4498 crosses Gisburn viaduct on the Blackburn to Hellifield line with a Manchester Victoria–Carnforth train on Saturday 28 March 1987. The A4 Pacifics were designed by Gresley and introduced in 1935. There were originally thirty-four locomotives in the Class and six examples survived into preservation. These include one in the USA, No. 60008 *Dwight D. Eisenhower,* and one in Canada, No. 60010 *Dominion of Canada.*

Hellifield, junction for the Blackburn line and the line from Skipton in West Yorkshire, is our next location as Tyseley's LMS Jubilee 4–6–0 No. 5593 *Kolhapur* pulls into the station on 21 March 1987 with the northbound 'Cumbrian Mountain Express' from Leeds to Carlisle.

LNER Class K1 2–6–0 No. 2005 and LMS Class 5MT 4–6–0 No. 5303 approach Settle Junction from Carnforth with the first leg of 'The Cumbrian Mountain Pullman' to Hellifield on 5 February 1983. On the right-hand side can be seen the S&C line from Carlisle. Until the mid-1980s, the Cumbrian Mountain trains were nearly always run in two legs, either Carnforth to Hellifield and then on to Carlisle, or the reverse. This of course required two sets of locomotives. On this occasion, the Hellifield to Carlisle section is being worked by Midland 'Compound' 4–4–0 No. 1000 and Jubilee 4–6–0 No. 5690 *Leander*.

On 20 September 1984, *Flying Scotsman* climbs Giggleswick bank with the second leg of the southbound 'Cumbrian Mountain Express' from Hellifield to Carnforth, the Carlisle to Hellifield section having been worked by LMS Coronation Pacific No. 46229 *Duchess of Hamilton*. This shot has changed somewhat, for where the photographer is standing is now the Settle bypass.

Opposite: 7F 2–8–0 No. 13809 gives off a fine exhaust as it climbs past Bentham with the Carnforth to Hellifield section of the northbound 'Cumbrian Mountain Pullman' on 30 April 1984. The second leg from Hellifield to Carlisle was worked by ex-SR West Country Pacific No. 34092 *City of Wells*. No. 13809 (BR No. 53809) was one of a batch of locomotives built in 1925, and was a development of a design by Henry Fowler of the Midland Railway for use on the Somerset & Dorset Joint Railway. The original Fowler engines had smaller boilers, and were introduced on the S&DJR in 1914. Note the locomotive is carrying a 22C shed code plate, the code for Bath used by the LMS from 1935 until 1950 after nationalisation, when the shed passed to the Southern Region control. This engine was privately preserved at the Midland Railway Centre at Butterley.

During the 1980s, this house adjacent to Capernwray viaduct, situated to the east of Carnforth on the line to Hellifield, must have seen many steam specials pass it by. Here on 15 May 1982 No. 4472 runs over the solid-looking viaduct with the bottom leg of 'The Cumbrian Mountain Express' bound for Hellifield, the second section to Carlisle being worked by SR 4–6–0 No. 777 *Sir Lamiel*. As can be seen from the previous picture, and those of the S&C on pages 106–12, there was a wide variety of motive power used over the years.

It would have been very difficult to run all these 'Cumbrian Mountain' trains without the facilities offered by Carnforth, the former LMR locomotive shed (10A) which after the end of steam on BR became 'Steamtown'. On the evening of 10 April 1982, No. 46229 poses by one of the shed's two coaling towers. The shed building is on the left-hand side. The Coronation Class Pacific had earlier worked into Carnforth with a train from Leeds.

A busy scene at Carnforth on the morning of 30 April 1984 with 7F 2–8–0 No. 13809 getting ready to work a train to Hellifield and, on the right-hand side, LMS 4–6–0 No. 5407 in steam. Note also the industrial tank engine outside the locomotive shed.

Before steam specials returned to the S&C line in 1978, one of the busiest steam routes was Carnforth to Sellafield via the Cumbrian Coast. At Sellafield is a triangle on which the locomotives could be turned, and on the outward trip, trains would often stop at Ravenglass so that people could leave the train and spend some time on the popular 15-inch gauge Ravenglass & Eskdale Railway, and then be picked up on the return journey. But when the 'Cumbrian Mountain' trains became a regular occurrence in the 1980s, the coast route naturally ran fewer trains. Some trains still ran on this scenic route, as on 30 May 1987, when No. 4472 *Flying Scotsman* ran through Grange over Sands with a return Sellafield sightseers' trip and passed the northern end of Morecambe Bay. (*Pete Skelton*)

Ulverston, some 19 miles from Carnforth, is not only the birthplace of one of the world's funniest comedians – Stan Laurel – but also has a fine railway station built by the Furness Railway. On 25 August 1980, SR 4–6–0 No. 850 *Lord Nelson* enters the station with the northbound 'Lancastrian' which ran from Carnforth to Sellafield and back. Note the ornate ironwork and the glass station canopy over platform one. Also, on the other platform are members of The Sealed Knot, who on that day would be re-enacting the Battle of Furness nearby. (*Christina Siviter*)

On 27 December 1980, two 'Santa Special' trains were run up the coast route. The picture on the right shows LMS 4–6–0 No. 4767 as it climbs Lindal bank out of Ulverston on the outward journey of a Hull to Sellafield train. The second train that day (below) was from Carnforth to Sellafield and was hauled by *Lord Nelson*. No. 850 is seen here near Askham in Furness as it heads for Sellafield.

We are now on the Settle & Carlisle route, one of the most popular lines used in the 1980s. The all-Pullman train 'The Pennine Limited' has just run through Settle, and *City of Wells* is making a fine effort as it climbs the 1 in 100 at Sheriffs Brow with this northbound special to Carlisle on 1 July 1986. Note the 'wrong line' working, due to PW work on the line. (*John Cooper-Smith*)

With the return to main line working of ex-LMS Jubilee Class 4–6–0 No. 45596 *Bahamas* in the summer of 1989, the first trips of this locomotive over the S&C were eagerly awaited. On Thursday 10 August 1989, No. 45596 in BR green livery with a rake of maroon coaches create a scene from BR steam days as they climb out of Horton in Ribblesdale with a Hellifield to Carlisle train.

There are many viaducts on the S&C line but none grander than Ribblehead viaduct, which is 440 yards long and has 24 arches. 'Black Five' 4–6–0 No. 5407 and Jubilee 4–6–0 No. 5690 *Leander* cross Ribblehead (or Batty Moss) viaduct on 29 May 1982 with the northbound 'Cumbrian Mountain Express' (CME).

Some 2 miles north of Ribblehead viaduct is Blea Moor tunnel. On 7 April 1984, No. 34092 *City of Wells* works hard through the cutting at the southern approach to the tunnel with the northbound CME. On the left-hand side is a Midland Railway fixed distant signal. Throughout the decade, No. 34092 worked many of these trains and could be relied on to throw out plenty of 'clag'. *City of Wells* was built in 1949, and withdrawn at the end of 1964. It went to Barry scrapyard and from there to the Keighley & Worth Valley Railway, where it was beautifully restored to main line running condition.

The return to main line steam running of Coronation Pacific No. 46229 *Duchess of Hamilton* on 10 May 1980 appropriately coincided with the 'Cumbrian Mountain Express' trains. On one of its early runs over the S&C on 28 March 1981, No. 46229 is seen running through the lonely outpost of Dent station with the southbound CME. The semaphore signal blades have just been removed but the posts remain, as do the short siding and loop lines (which were removed in 1982). On the extreme right-hand side can be seen the snow fences, very necessary at this location. At an elevation of around 1,000 feet Dent is the highest station in England.

These two views show how wintry the weather can get on this line. The one above, taken at Garsdale (some 3 miles north of Dent) on 30 January 1983, shows No. 4472 with a southbound special train run in conjunction with the SLOA members' annual meeting at Carlisle. The train is in the Down platform to allow Up West Coast diversion trains to run through the station.

Below is the southbound 'Cumbrian Mountain Pullman' train, hauled by MR 4–4–0 No. 1000 and LMS 4–6–0 No. 5690 *Leander*, as it crosses Ais Gill viaduct and approaches Ais Gill summit on a very cold 10 February 1983.

A regular visitor to the S&C in the early 1980s was SR 4–6–0 No. 850 *Lord Nelson* seen here climbing up to Ais Gill summit with a Carlisle train on 27 November 1982. In the background, the patchwork shapes of the Cumbrian fells are accentuated by the use of a long lens.

We are now around 6 miles north of Ais Gill summit at Birkett Common, where northbound trains can take it easy on the run down to Kirkby Stephen, but southbound trains face a stiff climb of 1 in 100 up to Ais Gill summit. A4 Pacific No. 4468 *Mallard*, with a southbound special from Eaglecliffe via Newcastle, pauses for a blow-up at Birkett Common on 29 August 1988. In the background is the Eden Valley.

1984 saw a rare visitor to the line when the Scottish-based ex-LNER A4 Pacific No. 60009 *Union of South Africa* made several trips over the Settle & Carlisle line. On 31 March 1984, No. 60009 climbs the 1 in 100 into Kirkby Stephen station with a southbound CME. This locomotive was privately preserved at Markinch in Fife after withdrawal from BR service in 1966.

Over the years, several stations on the line have been closed but some, like this station building at New Biggin, have been bought and splendidly restored as private dwellings. Restoration work is well in hand as LMS 'Black Five' 4–6–0 No. 5305 hurries past New Biggin station on 10 May 1986 with a southbound special. In the distance can be seen the fine-looking occupation bridge, which is a distinctive feature of this section of the line.

Duchess of Hamilton beats a tattoo on Culgaith Crossing as it heads south with the CME on 28 March 1981. Behind the first carriage can be seen the upper part of the Midland Railway signal-box, which also controls the crossing. Just visible on the extreme left-hand side is the entrance to Culgaith tunnel, which is 661 yards long.

At Carlisle, the locomotives which ran on the S&C were serviced at Carlisle Upperby depot (formerly 12B in BR steam days). On the evening of Friday 6 January 1984, No. 46229 poses on Upperby shed. The following day, it worked the southbound CME to Hellifield.

Chapter Six
Yorkshire & the North-East

Heading south-east out of Hellifield Junction on 10 May 1986 is 4–6–0 No. 5305 with a Carlisle–Leeds train. This line is part of the old Midland Railway route from St Pancras to Carlisle, and once used by 'The Waverley Express' which ran from London to Carlisle and then on to Edinburgh by the Waverley route.

The scenery in this part of West Yorkshire between Hellifield and Skipton is not unreminiscent of some parts of the old Somerset & Dorset line. I think that this is borne out by this picture of S&D Class 7F 2–8–0 No. 53809 as it heads towards Skipton on the evening of 16 August 1986 with a Carnforth–Sheffield train, the return 'West Yorkshire Limited'. The location is near Otterburn, 2 miles south-east of Hellifield.

Some 6 miles north of Skipton is Bell Busk, which was a popular location with one of the 'greats' of railway photography – the late Bishop Eric Treacy. The unusual combination of LNER Class K1 2–6–0 No. 2005 and LMS Class 5MT 4–6–0 No. 5305 climb the 1 in 132 gradient at Bell Busk with a Leeds–Carlisle special on 26 July 1986.

'The West Yorkshire Limited' (see opposite) pulls out of the former MR station at Skipton on 16 August 1986 and heads for Carnforth with a train from Sheffield. Note the station canopies and the amount of trackwork still in use. As well as being on the Leeds to Carlisle main line, Skipton was also the junction for the line to Nelson and Burnley (to the south-west) and the line to Ilkley (to the east) off which ran the Grassington branch. Today, only part of the Grassington branch remains (freight only to Rylstone) and a section of the Ilkley line at Embsay has been privately preserved – this is known as the Embsay & Bolton Abbey Railway. Skipton also had a locomotive shed (10G) which was situated on the south side of the main line, west of the station.

The line to Bradford Forster Square leaves the Hellifield to Leeds line at Bingley junction, just north-west of Shipley. On 31 August 1981, *Flying Scotsman* climbs out of Bradford and heads for Skipton with the ECS of the return 'North Yorkshireman' to Carnforth. This train between Carnforth and Skipton ran mid-week during the summer of 1981, with the ECS being stabled at Bradford Forster Square station. Bradford Manningham shed (55F) was situated at this location on the east side of the line at the rear of the train. In the late 1950s, it had an allocation of around 25–30 locomotives.

Above: This view of Bradford Forster Square station was taken on 25 August 1981 and shows A4 No. 4498 *Sir Nigel Gresley* pulling out of the station with the ECS of the return 'North Yorkshireman' from Skipton to Carnforth.

On Sunday 26 April 1987, A4 Pacific No. 4468 *Mallard* runs through Marsh Lane cutting in the eastern suburbs of Leeds and heads for York and Scarborough with 'The Scarborough Flyer'. The train had earlier arrived at Leeds from York via Knaresborough and Harrogate, part of the popular 'York Circular' route (see page 131).

LMS Class 4P 'Compound' 4–4–0 No. 1000 approaches Micklefield junction on a misty day, 28 September 1983, with a BR special train from York to Rochdale and return (see page 95). These handsome Midland Railway 4–4–0s were designed by Johnson and introduced in 1902. No. 1000 is the only member of the Class to survive and is preserved at the National Railway Museum, York. The lines on the right-hand side run to Selby (for Doncaster) and Hull.

The maze of lines around the West Riding of Yorkshire saw various steam workings in the 1980s, including this picture taken at Castleford station on 27 February 1983. *Flying Scotsman* approaches Castleford and heads for York with 'The Flying Scotsman' train from Peterborough. This run was part of No. 4472's sixtieth year celebrations (see also page 43). *(Pete Skelton)*

We now move to South Yorkshire and the northern outskirts of the steel city of Sheffield. West Country Pacific No. 34092, complete with Golden Arrow regalia, climbs through Nunnery junction towards Attercliffe with a train from Derby to York and then on to Carnforth. The lines on the extreme left are to Worksop and Lincoln. This 'John Player Special' train ran on 6 August 1988. (*John Cooper-Smith*)

Still in the outskirts of Sheffield, this time at Attercliffe, just north of the previous location, No. 4498 *Sir Nigel Gresley* heads through the station on 6 February 1988 with the Derby–York train. (*Robin Stewart-Smith*)

The ten-coach 'White Rose' special from Birmingham to York, hauled by LMS Jubilee 4–6–0 No. 5593 *Kolhapur*, gets into its stride near Wincobank station junction (near Tinsley) some 5 miles north-east of Sheffield. On the extreme right-hand side can be seen the line to Chapeltown.

A glorious sight in the town where it was built in February 1923, and also the first locomotive to be completed at Doncaster Works after the grouping, A3 Class 4–6–2 No. 4472 *Flying Scotsman* leaves Doncaster on a wet 27 February 1983 with 'The Flying Scotsman' sixtieth anniversary special from Peterborough to York. Such was the demand for tickets for this train that repeat trips were run on the following two Sundays. No. 4472 was not named in 1923, but during the following year, when it appeared in the 1924 Wembley Empire Exhibition (see also pages 43 and 118).

The original East Coast Main Line from Doncaster to York ran through Selby and Chaloners Whin junction. However, not long after this picture was taken on 5 March 1983, the Selby to Chaloners Whin section of the ECML was closed and a new line put in to the west of Selby, from Colton junction (5 miles south of York) to Doncaster via Temple Hirst junction (on the ECML north of Doncaster), thus avoiding the bottleneck at Selby where the busy Leeds to Hull line runs through.

No. 4472, with a Great Eastern No. 1 saloon and two Carnforth/Steamtown coaches, crosses the swing bridge over the River Ouse at Selby with a York to Peterborough train, prior to running the second of the 'Diamond Jubilee' special trains from Peterborough to York the following day. Note the overhead signal-box.

The next location is Gilberdyke Junction on the Leeds–Selby–Hull line. SR Class N15 4–6–0 No. 777 *Sir Lamiel*, which was restored by the Humberside Locomotive Preservation Group and shedded at Hull, approaches Gilberdyke Junction station on 29 December 1982 with a Manchester–Hull–Scarborough train. The line coming in from the left-hand side is from Goole and Doncaster.

Mallard makes a fine sight between the attractive display of semaphore signals at Gilberdyke Junction station with a York–Scarborough–Hull–Selby–York train on Wednesday 9 July 1986. The train will gain the ECML to York just to the west of Selby at East Hambleton junction. (*Pete Skelton*)

Hull Paragon station makes a splendid background as 4–6–0 No. 5305 pulls out of the former LNER terminus on 29 December 1982 with a special train to Scarborough. The first leg from Manchester had been worked by No. 777 (see page 124). This classic station was designed by G.T. Andrews for the York & North Midland Railway, and was opened in 1848. In its heyday it had fourteen platforms, but by the mid-1990s these were reduced to eleven, also with the loss of most of the platform canopies.

Beverley on the Hull, Driffield, Bridlington & Scarborough line is our next location. On 23 March 1982, *Sir Lamiel* pauses at Beverley during a test trip from Hull to Scarborough (and return). At the rear of the train can be seen the station with its overall roof, and on the right is Beverley Minster. Beverley was also the junction for the line to Market Weighton. (*David Eatwell*)

Driffield, some 11 miles south of Bridlington, was also the junction for the line to Malton (on the Scarborough to York line) and Market Weighton (on the Beverley to Selby line). On 9 July 1987, No. 4468 pulls through Driffield station and heads for Hull with a special charter train.

We leave the Bridlington line but not No. 4468. *Mallard* is seen just south of York on the ECML heading north with a Scarborough train on 25 April 1987. As you can see, electrification of the line is in progress, with some of the poles for the overhead catenary gantries now in place.

A classic picture at York as LNER A4 Pacific No. 4498 pulls out of the handsome station with the 'The West Yorkshire Enterprise' on 22 September 1984. This train ran from Leeds to Hull and then on to Scarborough, and returned to Leeds via York. Overlooking the scene is the beautiful medieval York Minster. Today, this view is all overhead wires and catenary. (*Hugh Ballantyne*)

The holder of the world speed record for a steam locomotive, LNER Class A4 Pacific No. 4468 *Mallard*, looks really at home as it waits to leave York station on 9 July 1986 on its inaugural return to steam run to Scarborough, Hull and then back to York via Selby and the EMCL (see also pages 124 and 126). This locomotive is preserved at the National Railway Museum. Note that the two centre through roads in this picture have now been removed.

Another of the National Railway Museum's fine fleet of locomotives, GWR 4–4–0 No. 3440 *City of Truro*, pulls out of York station on 4 September 1988 with the afternoon 'Scarborough Spa Express'. Although this is a North Eastern station, the Great Western locomotive seems perfectly suited to this cathedral of steam.

Opposite: On 28 August 1981, A3 Pacific No. 4472 rounds the tight curve at Kirkham Abbey with an afternoon York to Scarborough train. This location is 15 miles from York and 27 from Scarborough, and at one time there was a station here, but this has long since closed. The only intermediate stations now left on the line are at Malton and Seamer (junction for the Bridlington and Hull line).

No. 3440 again on a York–Scarborough train, this time at speed just north of Malton with the 1415 from York on 10 August 1986. Note the fine rake of Great Western chocolate and cream carriages.

LNER Class V2 2–6–2 No. 4771 *Green Arrow* has just pulled out of Scarborough station on 27 July 1986, with a return 'Scarborough Spa Express' for York. It is framed by the impressive gantry signal by Falsgrave signal-box. The gantry is NER with LNER type dolls and fittings. Just south of this location, a turntable was installed to cater for these popular trains.

We now return to the EMCL at Skelton junction, just north of York station, where on 7 October 1981 Midland Railway Class 4P 4–4–0 No. 1000 is about to leave the ECML and take the York Circular line to Harrogate and Leeds with a special train chartered by the Ford Motor Co. (*Pete Skelton*)

In the early to mid-1980s, the York Circular route (York, Harrogate, Leeds, York) was a popular line for steam specials. In the summer of 1982, regular trains were run on this route, with the addition of a York to Scarborough return trip. On 31 August 1982, No. 777 *Sir Lamiel* runs over the attractive viaduct over the River Nidd at Knaresborough en route to Harrogate and Leeds with a York Circular/Scarborough train.

During the 1980s, there were very few steam specials on the main line between York and Newcastle. However, on Sunday 17 August 1986 special trains were run from Newcastle via Sunderland and the coast route to Middlesbrough and on to Saltburn and return to Newcastle. Opposite, top, shows the 0900 departure from Newcastle to Saltburn as it heads through Seaton Carew (just south of Hartlepool) with LNER Class K1 2–6–0 No. 2005 in charge. After arrival at Saltburn, the K1 ran back to the triangle at Eaglescliffe North junction to turn. Note the three-masted sailing ship in the background, and on the extreme right-hand side the edge of the North Sea. The next scene (opposite, bottom) shows the previous train as it runs just east of Middlesbrough towards the coast resort of Saltburn on Sea. In the background is the unique Newport transporter bridge. The final scene shows the afternoon Newcastle to Saltburn train as it heads south across the Monkswearmouth Bridge over the River Wear at Sunderland. Note also the parallel road bridge.

Above and top: I mentioned earlier that steam specials were very rare on the ECML. However, on Sunday 21 June 1987, the day after working a series of special trains for the Tay Bridge centenary, V2 No. 4771 ran a special charter train from Edinburgh to York. Twilight is beginning to descend as the train eases off the King Edward Bridge at Newcastle and heads down the ECML to York. Just above the second span of the bridge (from the right) can be seen the roof of Newcastle Central station. In the foreground is part of the loop line from Central station via the High Level Bridge. A few hours earlier, No. 4771 with the Edinburgh to York special train was photographed crossing the famous Border Bridge at Berwick-upon-Tweed.

On Saturday 6 June 1981, a series of four special trains were run between Newcastle and Hexham to celebrate the 200th anniversary of the birth of George Stephenson on 9 June 1781. LMS 'Black Five' 4–6–0 No. 4767 *George Stephenson* pulls out of Newcastle Central station and threads the famous diamond crossing with the midday train to Hexham. This location has changed over the intervening years, with the outer platforms and track (off the right-hand side) being removed and the area now used for car parking. Also, with the electrification of the ECML, the view is rather obscured by catenary and wires.

Two views showing the evening departure from Newcastle to Hexham. Above is No. 4767 and the train to Hexham as it starts to cross the High Level Bridge. On the right-hand side above the bridge can be seen the Castle Keep, from where the previous picture of Newcastle Central station was taken. Left, No. 4767 is seen on the High Level Bridge framed by the span of the adjacent road bridge. Both the midday and evening trains to Hexham ran via the High Level Bridge and Norwood Junction, but the morning and afternoon trains ran via the Scotswood line, gaining the Newcastle–Carlisle line at Blaydon.

No. 4767 runs by the side of the River Tyne at Blaydon with the first of the four special trains to Hexham. (*John Cooper-Smith*)

The end of the outward journey for No. 4767 and the afternoon special from Newcastle, as it rolls into Hexham station on 6 June 1981. Note the North Eastern overhead signal-box and the very high lattice post semaphore signal for sighting purposes.

Just west of Wylam, some 12 miles east of Hexham, was where the line from Scotswood joined the Newcastle to Carlisle line. This section of line closed in the 1970s. On 22 January 1983, K1 2–6–0 No. 2005 hurries past the site of the former junction with a Middlesbrough to Hellifield charter train via Newcastle and Carlisle.

Having taken a water stop, No. 2005 is seen leaving Haltwhistle for Carlisle with the train in the previous picture. This station was the junction for the branch line to Alston, which crossed the viaduct on the right-hand side of the picture. This branch closed in 1976, but happily on the trackbed of the line between Alston and Kirkhaugh there now runs a very fine miniature railway, the South Tynedale Railway. Just through the smoke on the right-hand side of the station footbridge can be seen the elevated signal-box; note also the old water pump on the platform end.

Chapter Seven

Scotland

This section on Scottish steam starts in the south-west at Ayr where, on Saturday 11 November 1983, No. 4472 pulls out of the carriage sidings ready to haul 'The Sou'Wester Express' to Carlisle via Dumfries. (*David Eatwell*)

On 20 April 1985 'The Thames–Clyde Express' was run from Glasgow to Leeds via the GSWR route to Carlisle and then the Midland Railway S&C line to the Leeds area. LMS Jubilee Class 4–6–0 No. 5690 *Leander* darkens the sky and climbs up the 1 in 175 to Polquhap summit between Auchinleck and Kirkconnel and heads for Dumfries and Carlisle with the nine-coach special. After a break at Carlisle for servicing and so on, No. 5690 then hauled the train to Leeds via the S&C. (*Keith Jackson*)

Still on the west side of Scotland, but now on the North West, on the beautiful Fort William–Mallaig line. Steam returned to this popular route in the late spring of 1984 and then ran throughout the summer of that year, and has continued to run each summer ever since. During the very first week of steam operation, on Monday 28 May 1984, North British Railway 0–6–0 No. 673 *Maude* climbs the 1 in 50 gradient up to Glenfinnan station with a Fort William–Mallaig train – 'The West Highlander'. (*Pete Skelton*)

Two years later, and the motive power on the West Highland line is provided by ex-LMS 'Black Five' 4–6–0 No. 44767 as it heads away from the famous concrete Glenfinnan viaduct with 'The Royal Scotsman' from Fort William to Mallaig, 4 June 1986. This Wednesdays-only train was part of a Scottish Grand Tour train, one of the highlights obviously being this steam-hauled section.

In 1987, LNER Class K1 2–6–0 No. 2005 was on duty on the Fort William–Mallaig line, and is seen here near Fassfern heading for Mallaig with the (Wednesdays-only) 'Royal Scotsman' on 29 July 1987. Note the first three vintage carriages.

The summer of 1989 saw the Fort William trains in the hands of ex-LNER Class K4 2–6–0 No. 3442 *The Great Marquess*. This class was introduced in 1937, and No. 3442 was one of only six engines built. With their 5ft 2in driving wheels, they were designed for working on the steeply graded West Highland route between Glasgow and Fort William, and from 1949 they regularly worked on the Mallaig extension.

On 27 July 1989, *The Great Marquess* climbs through the mountains west of Lochailort with the 1035 Fort William–Mallaig train. At the time, this handsome engine was owned by the Earl of Lindsey, and was preserved at the Severn Valley Railway, Bridgnorth. Sadly, the Earl died shortly after this event, having fulfilled his wish to ride on his engine in the Highlands.

The Great Marquess again, this time in the dramatic setting of Loch nan Uamh viaduct near Glen Beasdale. No. 3442 crosses the concrete viaduct on 23 July 1989 with the 1645 from Mallaig to Fort William.

K1 2–6–0 No. 2005 crosses over the River Lochy as it pulls out of Fort William and heads for Mallaig on a damp-looking day, 28 July 1987. At the back of the train can be seen the diesel depot where the steam locomotives are also serviced and maintained. In the background can be seen the lower slopes of Ben Nevis, which at 4,406 feet is the highest mountain in the British Isles.

The steam workings on the Fort William–Mallaig line usually meant steam positioning trains to and from Glasgow to Fort William prior to the summer workings, or at the end of the summer/early autumn. On 17 October 1987, 'Black Five' 4–6–0 No. 5305 and a Fort William–Glasgow positioning special are seen in a wonderful West Highland setting as they climb the 1 in 55 up to County March summit, 1,024 feet high, 6 miles south of Bridge of Orchy. Dominating the scene is Ben Dorain at 3,524 feet high. (*John Cooper-Smith*)

A brief trip down the ECML as 0–6–0 No. 673 *Maude* passes Craigentinny carriage sidings on the outskirts of Edinburgh with an Edinburgh Circle train, run in connection with the annual 'Jazz Week', 5 June 1986. In a short distance, the train will leave the ECML at Portobello junction and take the Circle route back to Edinburgh Waverley station via Niddrie West junction, Gorgie junction and Haymarket Central junction.

Apart from odd trips like the one above, the popular Edinburgh Circle trains were usually run on weekends around the Christmas period. On a cold and frosty Sunday 14 December 1986, No. 673 climbs up to Niddrie West junction from the Portobello direction with a westbound 'Santa Special' Circle train.

On 11 December 1988, 2–6–0 No. 2005 heads eastwards at Niddrie West junction with an Edinburgh Circle train. The line on the left-hand side leads to Millerhill Yard. The hills in the background are Arthur's Seat, beyond which is the City of Edinburgh.

Although this locomotive is in LNER livery and numbered No. 2005, it was actually built for BR by the North British Locomotive Co. Ltd in June 1949, and its BR number was 62005. It was preserved by the North Eastern Locomotive Preservation Group (NELPG) at the North Yorkshire Moors Railway, Grosmont.

LNER Class D49 4–4–0 No. 246 *Morayshire* runs through the eastern end of Edinburgh Waverley station on 11 May 1983, on its way back to the SRPS depot at Falkirk, via Craigentinny and the Circle route. The locomotive had earlier worked a private charter train from Waverley to Rosyth.

The western end of Waverley station is the setting as No. 2005 leaves the outer platform with a Circle train on 11 December 1988. Above the rear of the train is the road which runs over the station and connects with the world-famous Prince's Street.

Ex-LNER A4 Pacific No. 60009 *Union of South Africa* runs through Prince's Street Gardens and heads for Waverley station with a train from Perth on 5 July 1986. This classic setting has now been drastically altered with the advent of electrification. (*John Cooper-Smith*)

There are two rail routes from Edinburgh to Perth, either through Polmont junction and Stirling, or through Dalmeny, the Forth Bridge and Ladybank, Ladybank also being the junction for the line to Dundee. This picture, taken at the southern end of the Forth Bridge at South Queensferry on the early morning of 1 October 1983, shows the unmistakable shape of A4 Pacific No. 60009 as it runs towards Edinburgh in order to take out the special charter train to Aberdeen via the Forth and Tay bridges.

This impressive view, photographed on the Forth Bridge itself (by permission of BR), shows *Union of South Africa* crossing the mighty bridge on 13 September 1980 with an Edinburgh–Perth special train. The bridge, which is almost 2 miles long, was opened in 1890. (*John Cooper-Smith*)

The first station after the Forth Bridge on the Ladybank route is Inverkeithing, which is also the junction for the line to Cardenden. On 5 May 1980, a series of shuttle trains were run between Edinburgh Waverley and Inverkeithing – 'The Fife Coast Express'. 0–6–0 No. 673 *Maude*, after arriving at Inverkeithing with the afternoon special from Edinburgh, is seen leaving the station at Inverkeithing in order to turn on the nearby triangle prior to returning to Edinburgh Waverley.

We leave the Ladybank line and take a look at the route from Edinburgh to Perth via Polmont junction (on the Edinburgh to Glasgow line) and Stirling. Class D49 No. 246 climbs the 1 in 100 out of Falkirk Grahamstown (near Laurieston), on 11 May 1983, with a private charter from Falkirk to Edinburgh (via the Edinburgh suburban circle route) and then on to Rosyth via the Forth Bridge. Note the first carriage is an LNER buffet car.

A4 Pacific No. 60009 *Union of South Africa* makes steady progress as it climbs the 1 in 88 gradient out of Dunblane with an Edinburgh to Perth and Aberdeen charter train on 18 April 1981.

The ECS of the privately chartered 'EMI Music Express' from Edinburgh to Gleneagles (the train originated at Kings Cross) heads for Perth to stable the stock and service the locomotives. The location is Dunning, some 8 miles south of 'The Fair City', on 7 April 1986. Hauling the train is the rare combination of LNER V2 2–6–2 No. 4771 *Green Arrow* and BR Standard Class 9F 2–10–0 No. 92220 *Evening Star*. This was the first appearance of a 9F in Scotland since the end of BR steam there – some twenty years previously. Note the semaphore signal with Caledonian Railway type post.

No. 60009, having taken water at Perth (see previous page), crosses the River Tay at Perth and heads for Dundee and Aberdeen on 18 April 1981. The two types of railway bridge make an interesting contrast, with the older one on the left having been built by Telford.

LNER 4–4–0 No. 246 *Morayshire* leaves Dundee and heads for Perth with a Falkirk–Edinburgh–Dundee–Perth–Edinburgh special train – 'The Taysider' – on Sunday 7 September 1980. On the right-hand side viaduct is the line to Edinburgh via the Tay Bridge, Ladybank junction and the Forth Bridge.

The centenary of the Tay Bridge was in 1987, and to celebrate the occasion on 20 June of that year, a series of shuttle trains were run over the famous 2-mile long bridge, which runs between Dundee and Wormit. The locomotive in charge of the Tay Bridge specials was appropriately LNER V2 *Green Arrow*, seen here approaching Wormit from Dundee on that historic day.

On a wet 6 September 1980, No. 60009 tops the 1 in 60 climb out of Dundee at Camperdown junction and heads for Aberdeen with a train from Edinburgh (via the Forth and Tay bridges). Behind the impressive semaphore signal is Camperdown junction signal-box.

We say goodbye to the east-coast area and head for the north of Scotland via the Highland Railway main line between Perth and Inverness. Steam trips over this beautiful line are rare, but in the early 1980s one or two were run, including this one on 20 July 1981, when LMS 'Black Five' 4–6–0 No. 5025 is seen heading south near Dunkeld with a return special from Aviemore to Perth. By this date a turntable had been installed at the Strathspey Railway's Aviemore depot, thus avoiding a lengthy run to Inverness and back for turning. (*John Cooper-Smith*)

In 1982 another Perth–Aviemore–Perth special was run on 12 June. The special train, headed by No. 5025, climbs up to Druimuachdar summit (1,484 feet above sea level) with the return working to Perth. (*David Eatwell*)

As with the Highland main line from Perth to Inverness, steam specials were rare on the former Highland Railway line from Inverness to Kyle of Lochalsh. However, throughout the week commencing 4 October 1982, a series of special steam excursions were run to the Kyle for the Toyota Car Co., motive power being 4–6–0 No. 5025 from the Strathspey Railway. On Monday 4 October No. 5025, plus support coach, approaches Inverness from Aviemore and runs under one of the magnificent gantry signals near Welsh's Bridge signal-box.

Turning round from the picture above, we see the rear of No. 5025 on the following day as it heads for the 'Far North' and Kyle platforms at Inverness station. In the background is the locomotive depot with Class 47s, 25s and 26s on shed. The scene is framed by Welsh's Bridge signal gantry and signal-box. With resignalling in the late 1980s, scenes like these are now a memory.

On the morning of Tuesday 5 October, No. 5025 pulls out of Inverness station and heads for Dingwall and the line to Kyle of Lochalsh. At the rear of the picture can be seen the platforms for the Edinburgh and Aberdeen trains, while coming in on the left-hand side are the through lines from these routes. To complete this scene is Rose Street signal-box, which controlled this busy area.

It is 0825 on the morning of 31 August 1986, and ex-LMS Class 5MT No. 44767 *George Stephenson* pulls out of the Highland capital of Inverness with a train to Helmsdale on the Wick/Thurso 'Far North' line. This was the first time for twenty-five years that steam had worked on this section of railway, and the main reason was to test out Radio Electric Token Block signalling (RETB) prior to its possible use on the steam locomotive workings on the Fort William–Mallaig line. The RETB system was in use north of Dingwall. By running this special train, it was possible to test the equipment in use on a steam locomotive, No. 44767 being fitted with radio aerials on the smoke box and on the tender behind the coal bunker.

No. 5025 arrives at Dingwall station on 5 October 1982 with a train for Kyle of Lochalsh. The junction for the Kyle line and the Wick/Thurso line is just a few hundred yards north of this attractive station. Note the platform canopies and buildings, also the fine Highland Railway footbridge, beyond which is the station signal-box, opposite the old goods shed.

After the junction at Dingwall, the Kyle line swings to the west, and 12 miles from Dingwall is the first station on the line, Garve. Entering Garve station on 5 October 1982 (see previous picture) is No. 5025 with the 'Toyota' special charter train for Kyle. The train returned to Inverness diesel hauled. No. 5025 travelled the 82½ miles back light engine tender first, there now being no turning facilities at Kyle.

On 5 October 1982 No. 5025 heads for Kyle of Lochalsh with the 'Toyota' train, and is seen near Attadale, to the west of Strathcarron.

Journey's end for No. 5025, photographed at Kyle of Lochalsh station after bringing in the special charter train from Inverness on 5 October 1982. I say 'journey's end', but the locomotive will now work back light engine and tender first to Inverness.

The special charter train to Helmsdale on 31 August 1986 is caught by the camera as it pulls away from Lairg and heads towards Helmsdale, with 4–6–0 No. 44767 in charge. (*John Cooper-Smith*)

The same train as in the picture at the bottom of page 159, only this time in more open country at Kirkton level-crossing, between Rogart and Golspie. In the background is the hill called 'The Mound', at the foot of which was once a junction station of the same name for the branch to the seaside resort of Dornoch, which in the late 1950s was worked by a Great Western Railway pannier tank. The GWR seemed to get everywhere!

The most northerly location that steam visited in the 1980s. Ex-LMS 'Black Five' No. 44767 runs round its train at Helmsdale, prior to returning with the special to Inverness, a journey of 101½ miles tender first, on the late afternoon of a (by now) very wet 31 August 1986.